ALTERNATIVE
CHICAGO

ALTERNATIVE CHICAGO

Unique Destinations Beyond the Magnificent Mile

BILL FRANZ

Cumberland House
Nashville, Tennessee

Published by Cumberland House Publishing, Inc., 431 Harding Industrial
Drive, Nashville, TN 37211-3160.

Cover design: Unlikely Suburban Design
Cover art: Dan Brawner
Interior design: Mary Sanford

Library of Congress Cataloging-in-Publication Data
Franz, Bill (William), 1967–
    Alternative Chicago : unique destinations beyond the Magnificent Mile /
    Bill Franz.
        p. cm.
    Includes index.
    ISBN 1-58182-090-9 (pbk. : alk. paper)
        1. Chicago (Ill.)--Guidebooks.   I. Title.

    F548.18 .F73 2000
    917.73'110443--dc21

                                                        00-022282

Printed in the United States of America
2 3 4 5 6 7—05 04 03 02 01

To my wife, Yanti,
for putting up with
my many addlepated
schemes and notions

A Guide to the Symbols in This Book

 Bar/Club

 Books/Magazines/Comics/
'Zines/Posters

 Clothing

 Coffee

 Food

 Furniture/Knickknacks

 Head Shop/Tattoo
Parlor/Hippie Hangout

 Liquor Store

 Live Music/Theater/
Performance

 XXX Pornography/Sex Shop

 Records/Tapes/CDs/Music

 Shoes

 Videos (Rental/Purchase)

CONTENTS

Introduction   ix
Organization   3
Chicago: A Very Brief History   3

THE LOOP   9
RIVER NORTH   15
WEST TOWN   19
LOGAN SQUARE   47
CLYBOURN CORRIDOR   51
OLD TOWN   57
LINCOLN PARK   61
LAKEVIEW   71
BOYS TOWN   79
BELMONT AND CLARK   91
WRIGLEYVILLE   105
SOUTHPORT AVENUE   113
NORTH CENTER   117
ROSCOE VILLAGE   119
ST. BEN   123
LINCOLN SQUARE   127
RAVENSWOOD   131
ANDERSONVILLE   135
UPTOWN   141

KOREA TOWN   147
DEVON AVENUE   151
ROGERS PARK   155
SOUTH LOOP   161
GREEK TOWN   163
LITTLE ITALY   167
MAXWELL STREET   171
PILSEN   175
CHINA TOWN   181
LITTLE TUSCANY   185
BRIDGEPORT   187
LITTLE VILLAGE   193
HYDE PARK   195

Information   201
General Index   203
Category Index   208

INTRODUCTION

Unlike many guidebooks, this one is not going to tell you where to stay or how to get around the city, or even what particular sights you should see. There are already dozens of guidebooks that concentrate on those very subjects—one of which you probably already have. This guidebook won't tell you which fancy, expensive restaurants to frequent, or the ritzy boutiques in which to shop. Instead you get a neighborhood-by-neighborhood account of the places you want to know about—resale and vintage shops, record stores and bookstores, offbeat eateries and cool bars and clubs. Those regular guidebooks are impersonal at best; at worst they assume their readers are carrying around enough cash to finance a small, third world nation. Think of them as guidebooks for your parents. This is *not* your parents' guidebook. This guidebook is for younger, more discriminating folk. And when I say younger, I don't just mean in the chronological sense, but young at heart. You can be sixteen or sixty and still vastly appreciate this book. You don't have to be under thirty to appreciate unique, independently owned establishments—which is primarily what is covered here. You won't find out where the nearest Borders Books or Tower Records is located, but you will find local institutions like Bookworks and Hi-Fi Records. No Hard Rock Cafe or Planet Hollywood, but how about Clubfoot Lounge and Heartland Cafe? Never heard of these joints? Of course you haven't. Nor have you heard of Land of the Lost Vintage or Una Mae's Freak Boutique. These are all distinctly Chicago places, and that's what you'll find here—neighborhood by neighborhood.

ALTERNATIVE CHICAGO

ORGANIZATION

After quite a bit of inner debate, I decided the most organized way to present these various neighborhoods was to begin in that section of the city most visible to newcomers—the Loop. This is where all the skyscrapers and businesspeople cluster. Though you'll probably spend most of your time north of here, this is a convenient starting point. We will then proceed directly north, sweeping outward and up. It is, after all, the north side where you'll find most of Chicago's premiere shopping, eating, and carousing joints. After the north side is finished, we'll start in the South Loop and sweep downward. Though geographically larger than the north side, the south side—with the exception of Hyde Park—is primarily residential and "unhip." Whereas many north side residents are transplanted suburbanites and Midwesterners, south siders were generally born in the same neighborhoods in which they reside. Though the shopping opportunities are much more limited here than up north, you'll find the south side is very much worth the pilgrimage for its food. There are some excellent joints down here—as well as a few Chicago delicacies such as the Italian breaded-steak sandwich you won't want to miss.

CHICAGO—A VERY BRIEF HISTORY

Back in the 1600s, the present-day site of Chicago didn't have much to recommend it to your average human being. It wasn't much more than a windswept marsh on the shores of Lake Michigan; even the local Potawatomi Indians avoided it. In 1673, however, French explorers under Louis Jolliet and Jesuit priest Jacques Marquette made their way through the region, which the Indians called *Checagou,* meaning "the place of the wild onion." Jolliet thought this area would make a great site for a trading settlement. Ships from all over the world could

find a sheltered harbor in Lake Michigan, and from there trading boats could traverse the Chicago, Des Plaines, and Illinois
Rivers to the Mississippi and eventually reach New Orleans. Of
course, that was assuming that the canal Jolliet envisioned
between the Chicago and Des Plaines Rivers was ever built.
The muddy, five-mile portage boaters currently had to endure
was a major hassle.

Apparently no one shared Jolliet's vision for many years to
come. It wasn't until 1779 that mulatto trapper Jean Baptiste du
Sable become the first settler in the region, trading with the
Indians. A handful of other traders began arriving over the next
few decades, yet it wasn't until a U.S. government exploring
party canvassed the region that things began clicking. In 1827
Congress finally authorized the building of Jolliet's canal. By
1833 Chicago was incorporated as a town. That same year a
treaty was worked out with the Indians to get them to remove
themselves west of the Mississippi River. The Indians knew
only too well what would happen were they to refuse. Much
like Chief Blackhawk in northeastern Illinois the year before,
they eventually would have been removed by force.

From here it was only a handful of decades before Chicago
went from being a mud-choked, frontier outpost to one of the
world's leading grain, lumber, railroad, and meat-packing cen-
ters, gathering the riches of the west before sending them on to
New York and the rest of the world. Indeed, even the modern
futures market as we know it today had its origins here, devel-
oping out of the grain trade.

But if Chicago was something before the Great Fire of 1871,
it was really amazing what happened after almost the entire
city was razed to the ground. Within twenty years it was rebuilt
bigger than before, becoming the world's first skyscraper city.

Amid all the construction and industry, however, there
were undercurrents of unrest. Workers often labored under
appalling conditions and long hours, many of them living in
overcrowded slums crawling with rats and disease. Though the
influx of thousands of German immigrants had given rise to an
active labor movement and socialist party, wealthy industrial-
ists didn't exactly feel the need to listen to grievances consider-

ing they had a ready supply of cheap, immigrant labor to exploit. Chicago elections weren't exactly on the up-and-up either. Vote fraud, ballot-stuffing, and intimidating gangs of thugs loitering about the polling places were the order of the day. Socialists soon grew disenchanted with their hopes of success through politics and began turning to anarchism. Their demonstrations and declarations in various newsletters greatly troubled the wealthy; tensions continued to mount on both sides.

After a series of strikes and protests, a rally was held on May 4, 1886, in Haymarket Square. This was a nonviolent affair, as even Mayor Carter Harrison, who had attended the rally, would later testify. The mayor had left by the time the meeting was breaking up, and this was when the police chief sent in the troops. As riot police—pistols in hand—marched toward a clump of stragglers listening to the end of a speech, a bomb was thrown into their midst, scattering cops in all directions. In the ensuing chaos, the police opened fire, as did those workers who were armed. Seven cops died and sixty were wounded. There was never an official count of the casualties among the workers, but it is presumed they were about the same as those suffered by the police.

This incident was tragic enough, but the authorities soon made a travesty of it. Eight anarchist leaders were arrested for the incident and subjected to a farce of a trial. Seven of them were sentenced to hang—even though only two of them had actually been present at the scene. As the prosecutor declared: "These men are no more guilty than the thousands who follow them. Gentlemen of the jury, convict these men, make an example of them, hang them and save our institutions, our society." Despite worldwide protest, the seven were hanged less than a year later.

Not surprisingly, this incident hardly troubled the movers and shakers of Chicago. Business continued booming and strikers were easily replaced or beaten into submission as thousands upon thousands of destitute immigrants continued to pour into the city. More skyscrapers appeared and Chicago's downtown became a marvel to behold. This earned the city the distinction of hosting the World's Columbian Exposition of 1893—a decidedly non–politically correct celebration of the four hundred years of civilization Columbus had unleashed upon the Americas.

As the century turned, Chicago continued to grow, its factories and stockyards some of the world's busiest. The year 1920 brought Prohibition, and not long after Al Capone was running the underworld, giving the city such colorful events as the St. Valentine's Day Massacre of 1929. Capone was out of the picture by the early '30s, but unfortunately the Great Depression was hanging heavy over the city and country. Things didn't much improve until the hyper-production of World War II. In 1942 Chicago was the site of another somewhat infamous event. Enrico Fermi and his cohorts at the University of Chicago managed to achieve the world's first self-sustaining nuclear reaction. The residents of Hiroshima and Nagasaki are still applauding that one.

The middle of the twentieth century and 1955 ushered in the arrival of *Da Mare*. Mayor Richard J. Daley ruled the city with an iron fist, as many across the country realized during the '68 Democratic Convention. This event was a gleeful period for the Chicago Police, who had Daley's blessing to club and beat hippie demonstrators to their heart's content, not to mention a number of reporters, a priest or two, and many an average Joe and Jane who simply stumbled into the chaos on their way home from work.

Daley died in 1976, and before his son, Richard M., could permanently replace him in 1989, Chicago had its first (and only) female mayor, Jane Byrne, and its first African-American mayor, Harold Washington. Ol' Richey M. is firmly in place now, however, and doesn't look to be defeated any time soon.

Today, after a period of stagnation through the '70s and early '80s, Chicago is in the midst of another boom period. From manufacturing to banking to coffee-slinging, jobs are plentiful. Construction is also going bananas. In the neighborhoods close to downtown, new buildings are sprouting up like crazy. And this is good, because a city can never have enough generic condos and stripmalls, can it? Plus there is Michael

Jordan and the Bulls. Or at least there was. With the completion of the 1997–98 season and the retirement of coach Phil Jackson and MJ, who knows what's going to happen to the team? Fortunately, Chicagoans have plenty to boast about, whether it comes in the form of sporting prowess, civic pride, or the levels of corruption in which their aldermanic officials indulge. It may be true that Chicago is the "Second City," (or, more properly nowadays, the Third) but most Chicagoans will tell you that that designation is purely a technicality.

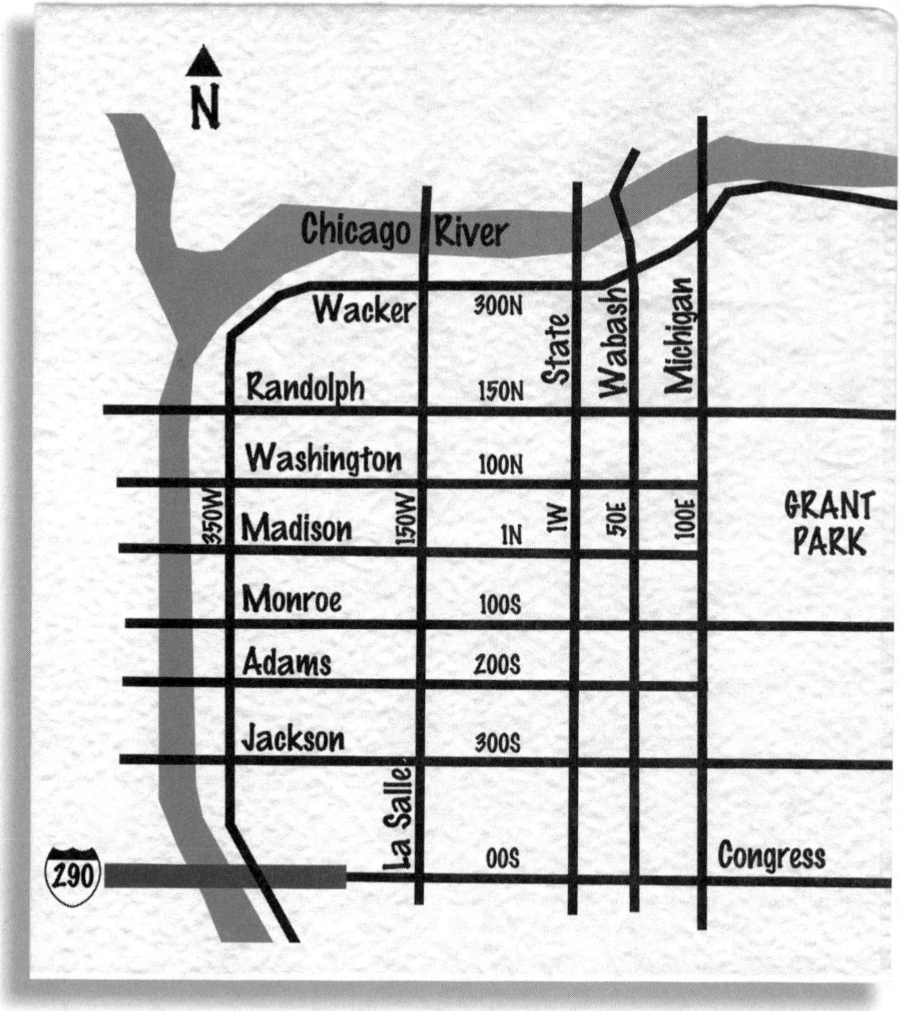

N
Chicago River
Wacker
300N
Randolph
150N
State
Wabash
Michigan
Washington
100N
350W
Madison
150W
1N
1W
50E
100E
GRANT PARK
Monroe
100S
Adams
200S
Jackson
300S
La Salle
00S
Congress
290

This is where Chicago sprang into the city it is now, growing up around a spot near the Chicago River called Wolf Point, near the massive Merchandise Mart at Wacker Drive and Lake Street. Today you can descend a flight of steps down to the riverbank and eat your lunch overlooking the spot where Mark Beaubien, an early tavern keeper, used to sit on his porch picking off ducks with his shotgun some 170 years ago.

From what was a hodgepodge assemblage of a few taverns in 1830 frequented by French trappers, Indians, and half-breeds, a real live city grew into being only ten short years later. Back then the Loop was the city limits, and all business was conducted in its confines, and the nearby neighborhoods were more like suburbs or small towns. By 1870 the Loop was known for its huge buildings, the appalling clouds of black smoke and soot hovering overhead, the crush of its wagon and railroad traffic, and its overcrowded mass of humanity. But then came the Great Fire of 1871, leveling the entire area. By 1890 it was completely rebuilt on a more massive scale then before, with several of the world's first skyscrapers making an appearance. The growth continued up until the eve of the

THE LOOP

Great Depression, and then it wasn't until the 1980s that it really picked back up again. The Loop now sports dozens of new skyscrapers, with more under construction.

The Loop—named after the loop of the elevated subway tracks—is where the city's banking and financial business is done, as well as most government activities. During rush hours and lunch times, nattily attired business folk—from receptionists to CEOs—dart about everywhere, filling the scores of eateries and coffee shops. You'll find a wide array of businesses here, most of them catering to big spenders. As far as food is concerned though, you can get anything from a gourmet meal to a cheap hot dog.

Within the Loop's confines are Grant Park along the Lake, the Art Institute on Michigan Avenue, and the Buckingham Fountain, along with several historical buildings like the Auditorium Theater, the Monadnock Building, and, of course, the Sears Tower. The Loop is very congested and parking is practically an impossibility, but you shouldn't leave Chicago without spending at least a few hours strolling about its streets.

BOOKSELLER'S ROW

408 S. Michigan Avenue 312-427-4242
Hours: Mon–Thu, 10:30 A.M.–8:30 P.M.; Fri–Sat,
10:30 A.M.–9:30 P.M.; Sun, 11:30 A.M.–7:30 P.M.

Though located in an area whose stores are not known for their bargains, Bookseller's Row is a good, general-selection, used book store with decent prices. On its three small floors, you'll find everything from art books and philosophy to sci-fi and self-help.

RAIN DOG BOOKS

404 S. Michigan Avenue 312-922-1200
Hours: Mon–Sat, 11 A.M.–6 P.M.; Sun, 12 P.M.–5 P.M.

If you'd like to step back for awhile into the "genteel world" of the old-school bookstore, this is your place. Rain Dog specializes in antiquarian books. Everything here is old, rare, and expensive.

THE SAVVY TRAVELER

310 S. Michigan Avenue 312-913-9800
Hours: Mon–Wed, 10 A.M.–6 P.M.; Thu, 10 A.M.–7 P.M.;
Fri–Sat, 10 A.M.–6 P.M.; Sun, 12 P.M.–5 P.M.

Here you'll find an outstanding collection of travel
books and maps for every region of the world, as well
as videos and a few CDs. They also sell travel accessories and luggage, along with a great collection of
photo books. Chicago's premiere place to hit if you're
planning a trip to somewhere a bit out there. They
even have detailed travel guides to Mongolia, for Pete's
sake!

CHICAGO ARCHITECTURE FOUNDATION

224 S. Michigan Avenue 312-922-3432
Hours: Mon–Sat, 9 A.M.–8 P.M.; Sun, 9:30 A.M.–6 P.M.

For those with an interest in architecture, this is a
place designed to make you go broke. They stock several great picture books and videos—not to mention
stained glass and various expensive models, knickknacks, and toys.

PRAIRIE AVENUE BOOKSHOP

418 S. Wabash Avenue 312-922-8311
Hours: Mon–Fri, 9:30 A.M.–5:30 P.M.; Sat, 10 A.M.–4 P.M.;
closed Sun

Another place for the architecture aficionado. This
store is dedicated solely to that medium. Here you'll
find plenty of picture books and biographies, but also
numerous books on theory as well as the technical and
administrative side of the business. They also have a
section upstairs devoted to rare and out-of-print
works, where you'll find several old Chicago city docu-
ments and plans.

EXCHEQUER PUB

226 S. Wabash Avenue 312-939-5633
Hours: Mon–Thu, 11 A.M.–7 P.M.; Fri–Sat, 11 A.M.–11 P.M.;
Sun, 11 A.M.–9 P.M.

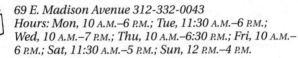

If you're looking for a decent place to drink in the Loop, I'd suggest the Exchequer Pub. It fills up with businesspeople and can get quite loud, but it's a nice, dim, old-style pub. They also serve up a damn good bowl of French onion soup.

COMIC RELIEF

69 E. Madison Avenue 312-332-0043
Hours: Mon, 10 A.M.–6 P.M.; Tue, 11:30 A.M.–6 P.M.;
Wed, 10 A.M.–7 P.M.; Thu, 10 A.M.–6:30 P.M.; Fri, 10 A.M.–
6 P.M.; Sat, 11:30 A.M.–5 P.M.; Sun, 12 P.M.–4 P.M.

One of the best comic stores in Chicago, Comic Relief stocks a huge selection of new comics and graphic novels—both mainstream, small press, and adult. Their collection of back issues is fairly large, and they also sell a smattering of models and toys as well as a few role-playing games.

U.S. GOVERNMENT BOOKSTORE

401 S. State Street 312-353-5133
Hours: Mon–Fri, 8:30 A.M.–4:30 P.M.; closed Sat and Sun

An interesting little shop where you'll find plenty of government reports and studies for sale. Many are indeed what you might expect—a cheaply put together report. Some, however—many of which are government-commissioned works put together by various foundations— are high-quality books. They also have a number of presidential addresses and national park guides.

AFROCENTRIC BOOKSTORE

333 S. State Street (Music Mart) 312-939-1956
Hours: Mon–Fri, 9:30 A.M.–6:30 P.M.; Sat, 10 A.M.–5 P.M.;
closed Sun

This small, sunny, attractive shop sells new books along with incense and greeting cards. The topics, of course, deal with African-American themes, and range from fiction to Christianity. The history section is particularly good, and they also have a great selection of conspiracy books.

CROW'S NEST MUSIC

333 S. State Street (Music Mart) 312-341-9196
Hours: Mon–Fri, 9 A.M.–8 P.M.; Sat, 9 A.M.–7 P.M.;
Sun, 11 A.M.–5 P.M.

Although Crow's Nest is a huge corporate store selling new CDs, cassettes, videos, and laser discs, you'll be surprised at the amount of quality stuff they have. All forms of music are well represented, with amazing back catalogs of even obscure groups like Negativeland. Though possibly a bit more expensive than you'd like, this place is still worth checking out for hard-to-find stuff.

LOOP RECORDS

302 S. Wells Street 312-663-4128
Hours: Mon–Fri, 9 A.M.–6 P.M.; closed Sat and Sun

A friendly, no-frills record shop, Loop Records has both new and used CDs as well as new cassettes and used vinyl. There's nothing spectacular among the albums—mostly '70s rock—but they do have plenty of budget CDs, a good hip hop section, and a number of music videos. A pleasant little place.

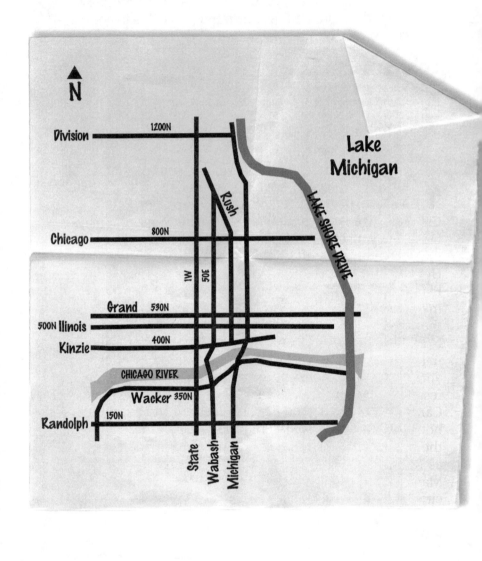

This is the city's hoity-toity section. Not only do Chicago's wealthiest folks live along Lake Shore Drive in an area known as the Gold Coast, but its premiere restaurants and shops also reside here. Heavies like Bloomingdale's and Water Tower Place set up shop on Michigan Avenue alongside many famous restaurants. Unfortunately, some of the famous restaurants in other parts of River North go by such familiar and heterogeneous names such as Hard Rock Cafe, Planet Hollywood, and Rainforest Cafe. Michael Jordan also has his restaurant in the neighborhood along with Harry Caray. Consequently, tourists flock here in droves, not so much interested in the sights as they are in the above-mentioned restaurants and places such as Navy Pier, Nike Town, and the Viacom Store. Many, sadly, never set foot in any other part of the city.

Not to knock River North. It's had its share of ups and downs, namely having all its homes and buildings razed to the ground alongside those of the Loop during the Great Fire. Only the historic Water Tower was left standing. But when the Palmers, a rich, influential family, went ahead and built their new mansion here in the 1880s, many a

RIVER NORTH

sycophant followed. Still, plenty of boarding houses and disreputable elements remained. This started to change after the construction of the Michigan Avenue Bridge in 1920. It wasn't until the late '40s, however, that the concept of the "Magnificent Mile" popped up—the term used to describe Michigan Avenue over the course of its journey north from the Loop to its end at Lake Shore Drive past Chicago Avenue. Though streets only a few blocks to the west, such as Clark Street, remained seedy all the way into the '60s, the entire area now, of course, is sparkling clean and wholesome—with the Gallery District having replaced the strip joints. Yet an argument can be made that a whiff of the seedy can still be found in the hopping, pseudo-upscale bars of the Rush/Division area—though that's probably just a matter of opinion. And of course the infamous Cabrini Green projects are only a stone's throw away. But don't worry, all those unsightly buildings will soon be knocked to the ground and replaced by $300,000 townhouses stocked with upstanding yuppie consumers. Where are the Cabrini Green residents going to go? Well, the developers haven't really figured that out yet—and don't appear to be giving it much thought either. Not when there are millions of fast dollars to be made right now in real estate and construction.

RAND McNALLY MAP & TRAVEL STORE

444 N. Michigan Avenue 312-321-1751
Hours: Mon–Sat, 9 A.M.–9 P.M.; Sun, 11 A.M.–7 P.M.

This is a small and expensive shop, but boy, it sure is cool. Here you'll find tons of guidebooks and maps, along with a number of small travel accessories such as current adapters and toiletries. They also sell an impressive collection of globes—which no household should be without, if for no other reason than to grow depressed at all the places in the world you'll probably never get to visit.

JAZZ RECORD MART

444 N. Wabash Avenue 312-222-1467
Hours: Mon–Sat, 10 A.M.–8 P.M.; Sun, 12 P.M.–5 P.M.

If you're into jazz, this is your place. They have a huge selection of jazz CDs—new and used—as well as plenty of vinyl. You'll also find very thorough sections on blues, folk, and international music, as well as boxed sets and videos. But don't come here if you're looking for the likes of Kenny G. The clerks won't only sneer, but will smack you as well.

AFTERWORDS

23 E. Illinois Street 312-464-1110
Hours: Mon–Thu, 9 A.M.–9 P.M.; Fri, 9 A.M.–11 P.M.; Sat, 10 A.M.–11 P.M.; Sun, 12 P.M.–7 P.M.

This new and used bookstore has a good general selection, with plenty of political books. In the basement you'll find the used stuff as well as a small cafe. The used books are displayed just as accessibly as the new ones and tend to be rather current. A good place to go if you're looking for a used copy of a book that hasn't come out in paperback yet.

ABRAHAM LINCOLN BOOKSHOP

357 W. Chicago Avenue 312-944-3085
Hours: Mon–Sat, 9 A.M.–5 P.M.; closed Sun

This place rocks! Though you have to be buzzed in and the general atmosphere is like that of a library what with the various portraits and paintings lining the walls, this place is not at all musty and stuffy like you might expect. The staff is very friendly and helpful and the stock is incredible. If you get excited about nineteenth-century American history—as I, admittedly, do—you'll go into raptures among the stacks. Lincoln and the Civil War are their specialties, with hundreds of books on those subjects, but you can find works on pretty much any and all topics of U.S. history, from the eighteenth century to the present. Also, if you're in the market for a replica of the Lincoln death mask—and who isn't?—they have plenty to choose from, one for every budget.

PIPPIN'S TAVERN

806 N. Rush Street 312-787-5435
Hours: Sun–Fri, 11 A.M.–4 A.M.; Sat, 11 A.M.–5 A.M.

Pippin's is a rarity in this part of town: a loud yet laid-back neighborhood pub with a widely mixed clientele. Rubbing elbows in this good-natured place you'll find tony Gold Coast types, students, construction workers, off-duty chefs, and many a shade in between. And you can't beat the free baskets of popcorn. The preferred place to drink in the neighborhood.

EUROPA BOOKSTORE

832 N. State Street 312-404-7313
Hours: Mon–Fri, 8 A.M.–10 P.M.; Sat, 9 A.M.–10 P.M.;
Sun, 9 A.M.–8 P.M.

Here you'll encounter a wide array of magazines, both domestic and foreign, as well as newspapers, foreign language books, and guidebooks. If you're European and have a hankering to see your own language in print, this is your place.

DR. WAX

1207 N. State Street 312-255-0123
Hours: Mon–Fri, 11 A.M.–9 P.M.; Sat, 11 A.M.–10 P.M.;
Sun, 1 P.M.–10 P.M.

Dr. Wax is a small Chicago chain with stores throughout the city. This particular one has plenty of new and used CDs along with a good discount bin. The selection is a decent mix of rock, R&B, and jazz. They even stock some new hip-hop vinyl as well as a smattering of rock-and-roll novelty items.

West Town is one of the more interesting areas of the city—and you'll probably want to spend quite a bit of time here. Originally a suburb of Chicago containing some impressive mansions, the area started declining around the 1920s. By the '40s it was a Polish ghetto. Nelson Algren wrote of this area in *The Man with the Golden Arm*. In fact, a portion of Division Street was called Polish Broadway due to all the bars and clubs along its length. Despite its heavy concentration of Poles, however, West Town is made up of several ethnicities and neighborhoods. Wicker Park, Bucktown, East Village, Ukrainian Village, Logan Square—all are within West Town. Lately these neighborhoods have gone through intense gentrification, with Bucktown foremost among them. My own earliest memory of Bucktown is not exactly pleasant. Years back when I was a teenager and self-proclaimed "punk rocker," some friends and I were attacked without warning by a gleeful band of youthful white hardasses. The chances of this happening these days are all but nil. Unless, perhaps, you manage to tap the bumper of the sport utility vehicle in front of you while parallel parking. Before you know it you may find yourself

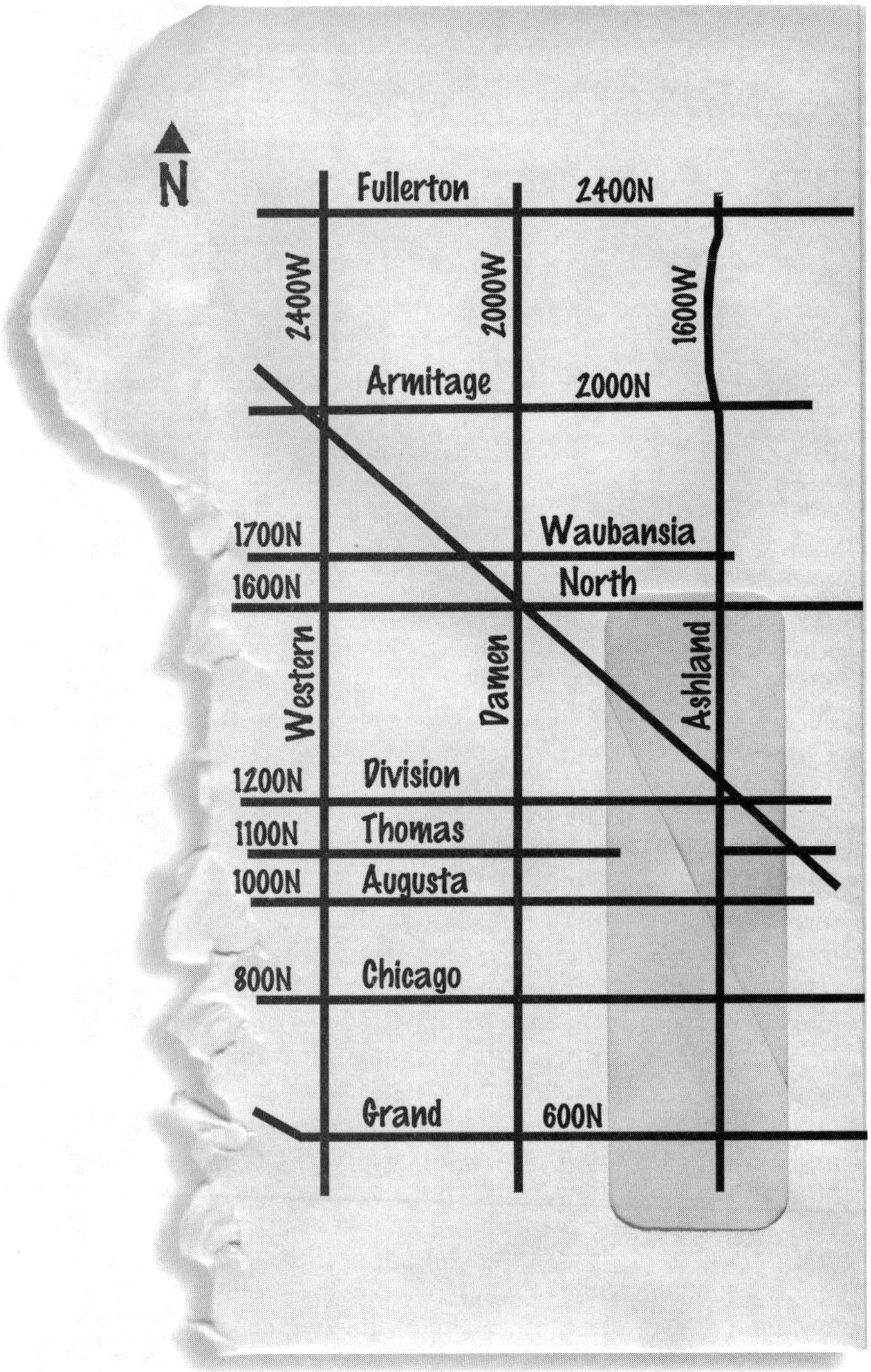
N
Fullerton
2400N
2400W
2000W
1600W
Armitage
2000N
1700N
Waubansia
1600N
North
Western
Damen
Ashland
1200N
Division
1100N
Thomas
1000N
Augusta
800N
Chicago
Grand
600N

under attack by a handsome yuppie family and their golden retriever, because although vestiges of the Mexican community are still present, Bucktown is a yuppie haven. They've bought houses and condos throughout the entire neighborhood. The shops are mostly expensive boutiques, and the restaurants are of the glitzy, trendy variety.

Wicker Park, right next to Bucktown, will soon be the same. Wicker's main intersection of Milwaukee, Damen, and North was a desolate, garbage-strewn eyesore only some ten years ago. Now the large Mexican and Polish communities that resided here—as well as the masses of artists—are being pushed out in favor of strip malls, condos, and yuppies.

The artists started the decline, as usual. Back in the '80s, space was dirt cheap in the neighborhood, but as more and more artists moved in, the inevitable slew of students and assorted hipsters followed. And yes, I was one of them. I lived in Wicker Park off and on from 1991 to 1997—except for a few stints in New Orleans. The neighborhood has drastically changed since I first arrived—in both its ethnic makeup and the character of its shops and eateries, but what else is new? This has been happening since the beginning of the city.

The other neighborhoods, such as East Village, are yielding much more slowly to change, but change is indeed making itself felt. More and more the young "artistes" are being driven into the cheaper, heavily Mexican areas, and the Mexicans, in turn, are being forced further west. Even Ukrainian Village—a respectable bastion of old world Ukrainians and Polish—is starting to bend. Years back a Brazilian friend of mine was looking for an apartment in the area. Though he is as white as George Bush, he ended up using his girlfriend's last name in dealing with landlords. Somehow the name of Pinto wasn't opening the right doors for him. That, however, isn't much of a problem these days, as you see plenty of young, mixed-race, hipster couples living in the neighborhood.

Now, you may be wondering why I've lumped all these seemingly separate neighborhoods into the convenient heading of West Town. The reason is simple. The boundaries of these areas are not too firmly fixed—at least not in the minds of the residents. In the course of one night's carousal in West Town, you may very well wander into every single one of these neighborhoods as you flit from place to place. Therefore, to impose some sort of order, I decided to lump businesses together not by neighborhood, but by street. Milwaukee Avenue, for example, is one of West Town's main arteries. It enters West Town in East Village and passes from Wicker Park and Bucktown into Logan Square (the latter an area I will deal with separately as it is "psychologically"—if not technically—outside of West Town). Chicago Avenue, on the other hand, enters in East Village and continues through Ukrainian Village, never hitting Wicker Park proper. Yet despite this, Chicago Avenue is as much a part of the Wicker Park "experience" as Milwaukee Avenue itself.

As I said at the beginning of this lengthy introduction, you'll probably be spending a lot of time in West Town. This region is second only to the Belmont/Clark area up north as Chicago's premiere hipster shopping district. You'll find plenty of vintage shops, and book and record stores, plus an immense slew of bars, clubs, and restaurants. Here also are plenty of Mexican discount shops and taquerias, as well as a number of Polish joints. It's not very hard to have a good time here. Much like that silken-voiced president of Men's Wearhouse, I guarantee it.

MILWAUKEE AVENUE

Entering West Town in East Village, you'll find one side of Milwaukee taken up by very well-kept, low-rise projects while various upscale, hipster businesses hold court across the street. Past the big intersection at Ashland and Division, you hit Wicker Park proper. Gentrification generally hasn't spread here yet; tacky furniture shops and dollar stores are in the majority. Soon enough, however, you're getting smack dab into it as you approach the intersection at Damen and North. On weekend nights this place is hopping, especially after 2 A.M. when everyone is headed to their favorite after hours bar.

North of the intersection used to be a quiet, industrial area. That is rapidly changing. Two insidious strip malls have appeared and with them new businesses like Blockbuster Video are sprouting up. After the intersection at Western, Milwaukee heads into Logan Square, where you'll find my favorite thrift store—Village Discount Outlet—written up in the Logan Square section.

BLACK MARKET CHICAGO

 1116 N. Milwaukee Avenue 773-278-6780
Hours: Mon–Sat,12 P.M.–8 P.M.; Sun,12 P.M.–6 P.M.

For the leather fetishist in all of us, Black Market provides all your S&M needs as well as lingerie, vibrators, sex toys, lubricants, etc. Despite the foreboding merchandise, this is a very friendly little shop. They can also outfit the well-dressed goth and provide plenty of printed literature if he or she is looking to specialize in a particular S&M field.

DUSTY GROOVE

 1180 N. Milwaukee Avenue (second fl.) 773-645-1200
Hours: Fri,12 P.M.–8 P.M.; Sat,12 P.M.–6 P.M.

This spartan, sunny record store is a great place to hit if you're looking for jazz and world music. They sell more old vinyl than new CDs, but as for the latter they have good current selections of hip hop, acid jazz, and various "drum & bass" compilations. Amid the reasonably priced vinyl you'll find plenty of old Latin and African albums.

ARK THRIFT SHOP

 1302 & 1308 N. Milwaukee Avenue 773-342-1504
Hours: Mon–Thu, 10 A.M.–6 P.M.; Fri, 10 A.M.–3 P.M.;
closed Sat; Sun, 10 A.M.–5 P.M.

Ah, the Ark empire. You'll find a few of these shops throughout the city. This two-location complex is a good place to find cheap furniture. The clothes selection is nothing special, but the bargain basement over at 1302 always makes for a good browse. Here you'll find the really cheap stuff, from chairs and tables to only slightly soiled mattresses and exercise equipment.

THREADS ETC.

 1400 N. Milwaukee Avenue 773-276-6411
Hours: Mon–Sat, 11 A.M.–7 P.M.; Sun, 11 A.M.–5 P.M.

 This is a fine, mid-sized resale/vintage shop with plenty of goods for both men and women. Standard shirts and pants fill the racks in front, while in the back room are plenty of jeans and footwear along with a few CDs and cassettes. The staff are friendly and are always more than willing to let you know if there's a special sale in effect.

BULLDOG RECORDS

 1420 N. Milwaukee Avenue 773-276-5817
Hours: Fri–Sat, 12 P.M.–8 P.M.; Sun, 12 P.M.–6 P.M.

 This large record shop specializes in new and used punk. CDs are the primary stock, but they do have a decent amount of new vinyl. But music is just one facet of the merchandise. You can also get posters, T-shirts, baseball caps, books, and fanzines. And that's still not all. Believe it or not, they stock one of the best collections of hot sauces in the city. Plenty of gourmet shops don't even carry these concoctions. Yee ha!

UNA MAE'S FREAK BOUTIQUE

 1422 N. Milwaukee Avenue 773-276-7002
Hours: Mon–Fri, 12 P.M.–8 P.M.; Sat, 11 A.M.–8 P.M.; Sun, 12 P.M.–7 P.M.

Despite the title, you won't find this place to be unusually freaky, but you will find plenty of decently priced, good quality vintage clothing for (mostly) women, as well as accessories made by local designers. They do have some never-worn stuff with original price tags. Of course, that doesn't mean you can purchase these items for the original cost. Life isn't that easy. This is a nicely appointed little shop.

ZAK'S TAVERN

1443 N. Elk Grove Avenue 773-235-9063
Hours: Sun–Fri, 11 A.M.–2 A.M.; Sat, 11 A.M.–3 A.M.

Places like Zak's are becoming more and more of a rarity in Wicker Park—a dim, slightly rundown, comfortable little joint catering to both the local art slob as well as the elderly local drunk. Prices are cheap, the atmosphere is low-key, it very rarely gets crowded, and hey, during basketball season you get to eat free hot dogs during Bulls games. It doesn't get much better than that.

EL CHINO

1505 N. Milwaukee Avenue 773-772-1905
Hours: Sun–Fri, 11 A.M.–4:30 A.M.; Sat, 11 A.M.–5 A.M.

Good old El Chino. What makes this place so popular is its willingness to remain open after 4 A.M. Once Nick's across the street starts itching to kick its patrons out for the night, El Chino reaps the benefits. Their food is, for the most part, nothing special—but it is cheap. While the chorizo tastes unlike any I've ever had—and I don't mean that in a positive way—the chips and salsa are very good, and the chicken quesadillas are pretty tasty as well, though oddly enough, they don't have any cheese in them. Go figure.

SALVATION ARMY THRIFT STORE

1515 N. Milwaukee Avenue 773-489-5194
Hours: Mon–Sat, 10 A.M.–6 P.M.; closed Sun

This Salvation Army branch is spacious but not particularly rewarding. You'll find a basic selection of clothes and shoes here along with dishes, knickknacks, and a bit of furniture. I should also mention that the books are worth picking through as you can occasionally find something decent.

NICK'S

1516 N. Milwaukee Avenue 773-252-1155
Hours: Sun–Fri, 4 P.M.–4 A.M.; Sat, 4 P.M.–5 A.M.

Nick's occupies the site of what used to be Club Dreamerz. Dreamerz was a bit of a legend in its time, yet even so you're not likely to find too many people—myself included—who are proud to admit that they used to hang out there. Nick's doesn't have this problem, I imagine. Having been shunted out of its ancestral home in Lincoln Park, Nick's was part of the first wave of more upscale joints that began to hit Wicker Park a number of years back. What was once a rather run-down bar with nasty bathrooms is now a very attractive, well-kept joint. Pool tables have filled the dance floor and the DJs have been replaced with a jukebox, but the place still fills up after 4 A.M. on Saturdays. Only now the crowd has a little less ennui and a lot more money. This is good in a way, as the prevalence of near-strangers trying to bum drinks off you pretty much disappeared with the demise of Dreamerz. A beer garden is open during the warmer months, but it's not the same as in the old days—it's no longer decorated with tombstones and huge, stark paintings of naked zombies. Oh well.

BACKSEAT BETTY'S

1530 N. Milwaukee Avenue 773-227-2427
Hours: Mon, 11 A.M.–7 P.M.; Tue–Sat, 11 A.M.–9 P.M.;
Sun, 11 A.M.–7 P.M.

Spanning the decades from the '20s to the '70s, Backseat Betty's is one of the best vintage shops in the area. This place has a very good selection of high-quality stuff—some of which was even put together by local designers. Though women will fare much better here than men, they do have a few items for those of us who belong to the coarser sex.

RECKLESS RECORDS

1532 N. Milwaukee Avenue 773-235-3727
Hours: Mon–Thu, 11 A.M.–9 P.M.; Fri–Sat, 11 A.M.–10 P.M.;
Sun,11 A.M.–8 P.M.

One of two stores the highly respected Reckless chain keeps in Chicago, this one has new, more spacious digs. Here you'll find an outstanding selection of new, used, and rare CDs, vinyl, cassettes, and videos, as well as a smattering of music mags and 'zines. Reckless also offers the best prices in the city if you're looking to sell off any old albums.

BIG HORSE

1558 N. Milwaukee Avenue 773-384-0043
Hours: Sun–Fri, 10 A.M.–2 A.M.; Sat, 10 A.M.–3 A.M.

Big Horse combines the best of the old Wicker Park in one cramped, smoky little den. In front is a genuine Mexican taqueria serving up burritos and nachos and all sorts of goodies, while in back you can drink anything from a small selection of imports to your typical cheap corporate brew while watching locals wail away on their instruments at the other end of the room. You can never be sure just what caliber of band might be playing here. You get anything from seasoned veterans doing a knockoff show for fun to kids who have never had an audience beyond their boyfriends and girlfriends. Though relatively new to Wicker Park, this place has quickly become an institution.

OCCULT BOOKSTORE

1561 N. Milwaukee Avenue 773-292-0995
Hours: Mon–Thu, 10:30 A.M.–7 P.M.; Fri–Sat, 10 A.M.–9
P.M.; Sun, 12 P.M.–6 P.M.

Once a resident of the Clark/Belmont area up north, the Occult Bookstore stocks a good collection of books on the arcane, metaphysical, and, of course, the occult. They also sell a large collection of publications along with incense and candles and such.

EARWAX

1564 N. Milwaukee Avenue 773-772-4019
Hours: Mon–Thu, 11 A.M.–12 A.M.; Fri, 11 A.M.–1 A.M.; Sat,
10 A.M.–1 A.M.; Sun, 10 A.M.–11 P.M.

Earwax quickly developed into a Wicker Park institution upon its arrival in the neighborhood several years ago—and has managed to retain that status despite the heavy competition that has sprung up around it over the past few years. Though there are at least three other coffee shops a stone's throw away in either direction, I figured I need only mention Earwax. The other places are fine, I'm sure, and you'll have no problem running across a number of them in the neighborhood, but Earwax definitely stands out. Primarily a coffee house serving up good grub (I've even had a decent mufaletta here once), this joint also serves as a book and music store, not to mention a video rental outlet. The selection of books and CDs is small but very good, while their stock of videos is exceptional. Everything from hard-to-find documentaries to foreign films and 70s exploitation—as well as high-quality Hollywood fare—can be found here. And you don't need a membership to rent, just a credit card and driver's license.

THE NOTE

1565 N. Milwaukee Avenue 773-489-0011
Hours: Sun–Fri, 8 P.M.–4 A.M.; Sat, 8 P.M.–5 A.M.

Relocated to the Flatiron Building, which has traditionally housed artists and their studios but has slowly been weaning itself of this heritage, The Note is a dim, cavernous, smoky space featuring very good jazz and funk acts as well as swing bands. Martinis and cigars are in abundance. The Note has retained its reputation from its former digs on Armitage (when it was called The Blue Note) as the place for the reasonably affluent and young to go after the 2 A.M. bars close.

DOUBLE DOOR

1572 N. Milwaukee Avenue 773-489-3160
Hours: Varies. Call ahead or check paper for times.

This is Wicker Park's only large venue for local and national bands. From relatively unknown locals to legends such as Pere Ubu, a wide gamut of bands plays here. Drink prices are high, but they do occasionally have specials. Downstairs you'll find a whole slew of pool tables, while in a little nook up a small flight of stairs from the main room, you'll find a comfortable lounging area. The interior of Double Door is very well done, and if you can kick back here on a night when it's not too crowded, it's a very comfortable place to see a band.

WICKER DOG

1589 N. Milwaukee Avenue 773-384-8505
Hours: Open every day 11 A.M.–4:30 A.M.

Wicker Dog is one of the hundreds of hot dog and burger shacks throughout Chicago, yet somehow their food is better than most. The fact that I usually find myself eating here after a long night of drinking may be influencing my opinion somewhat, but you have to give credit to the fact that they even make good greasy subs. Not very many similar types of joints can boast as much. Yet the gourmet item has got to be the fresh-cut fries. You can make a meal out of them alone. A great place to hit after the bars.

IRAZU

1865 N. Milwaukee Avenue 773-252-5687
Hours: Mon–Sat, 10 A.M.–9 P.M.; closed Sun

I used to live right near Irazu when it was a cramped little carry-out joint serving up their special Costa Rican burritos and specialties. Though they've fixed the place up some and added an outdoor patio, I'm pleased to say the food is the same great fare. Even in the old days this place was always filled with people waiting on food; now you'll have to wait a little longer, but it's worth it.

CHICAGO AVENUE

The East Village section of Chicago Avenue is still primarily Mexican, with furniture shops and various other such practical establishments. This continues past Ashland up to Damen Avenue. Now you're starting to get into Ukrainian Village. After Western you're soon in Humboldt Park, where, unfortunately, there's really not a whole hell of a lot going on.

CASEY'S

1444 W. Chicago Avenue 312-243-2850
Hours: Mon–Thu, 11 A.M.–9 P.M.; Fri–Sat, 11 A.M.–11 P.M.;
Sun, 12 P.M.–9 P.M.

One of my favorite liquor stores. Here in this friendly, neighborhood shop you'll find plenty of imported beers from all over the world, with many a Belgian ale to choose from. There are plenty of wines and spirits too, but beer is definitely the specialty. I can easily spend an hour browsing through the options. Much like Buck in *The Call of the Wild*, I fall into a trance thinking about the good beers I've drunk in the past and the beers I'd like to drink in the future.

ARK THRIFT SHOP

1505 W. Chicago Avenue 312-733-3314
Hours: Mon–Thu, 10:30 A.M.–7 P.M.; Fri, 10:30 A.M.–4 P.M.;
closed Sat, Sun, 10:30 A.M.–6 P.M.

Though the Ark usually means spaciousness and good selection, this one doesn't exactly live up to the famous Ark standard. At this particular Ark outlet, you'll find a small batch of serviceable clothes and only a smattering of furniture.

DEMAR'S

 1701 W. Chicago Avenue 312-666-4317
Hours: Mon–Sat, 6 A.M.–7 P.M.; Sun, 6 A.M.–6 P.M.

Something that is fast becoming a rarity in many parts of West Town: a genuine, dirt-cheap diner. From ridiculously low-priced breakfasts to edible sandwiches and dinner specials, Demar's is a no-frills, authentic relic of what is fast being replaced by expensive, stylized versions of the same.

AMERICAN THRIFT STORE

 1718 W. Chicago Avenue 312-243-4343
Hours: Mon–Sat, 11 A.M.–7 P.M.; Sun, 11 A.M.–5 P.M.

Though hot and muggy inside, this is a well-kept, orderly shop. Hanging from the many racks are all sorts of incredibly cheap, basic clothing. For items like T-shirts, sweatshirts, and button-downs, this is your place. (I must say, though, the pricing is a little odd. I once bought a sweatshirt here for $1.88. Not that I'm complaining of course, it's just not exactly a figure you're used to seeing at a resale shop.)

TECALITLAN

 1814 W. Chicago Avenue
Hours: Sun–Thu, 10 A.M.–12 A.M.; Fri–Sat, 10 A.M.–3 A.M.

 This Mexican restaurant not only provides a carry-out station to give you easy access to their excellent burritos and such, but they also have a spacious dining room and full-service bar. Their prices increased several years back when they remodeled, but they're still pretty reasonable and the food is worth it.

BLUE WILLOW

 1958 W. Chicago Avenue 773-384-6499
Hours: Open every day 11 A.M.–10 P.M.

A small, no frills, Chinese restaurant, Blue Willow is one of the few of its kind still remaining in the neighborhood. I wouldn't say the food is particularly outstanding, but it's good, decent fare at cheap prices.

POP'S ON CHICAGO

2053 W. Chicago Avenue 312-633-0828
Hours: Sun–Fri, 7 A.M.–2 A.M.; Sat, 7 A.M.–3 A.M.

As a music venue, Pop's is a relative newcomer to West Town. You'll find it a tattered, comfortable, down-to-earth place to see a local band or shoot some pool. The stage is not very big and the quality of the bands varies widely, but what the hell, there's never a cover and you can drink anything from Bass to Busch.

TUMAN'S ALCOHOL ABUSE CENTER

2159 W. Chicago Avenue No listed phone number.
Hours: Sun–Fri, 3 P.M.–2 A.M.; Sat, 3 P.M.–3 A.M.

With a decor unchanged since the '20s, Tuman's is the best of the old and new West Town. At the bar or about the pool table in back can be found many a neighborhood old timer swilling Pabst alongside the youthful hipster newcomers. This is an amiable, low-key little joint. And, oh yeah, you can get falling-down drunk for only $20.

KASIA'S POLISH DELI

2101 W. Chicago Avenue 773-486-6163
Hours: Mon–Sat, 9 A.M.–6 P.M.; Sun, 10 A.M.–2 P.M.

If you've got a hankering for some great pierogis or other Polish dishes, this is the place to go. They've got a huge, mouth-watering selection sitting under glass just waiting to slide down your grubby little gullet. The place isn't big enough for a dining area so you'll have to take your goodies and go, but if you speak Polish, make sure to chat awhile with the neighborhood ladies.

AUGUSTA BOULEVARD

Augusta is primarily residential and still heavily Mexican. A quiet, pleasant street, it hosts a few bars east of Damen before entering Ukrainian Village.

CLUBFOOT LOUNGE

1824 W. Augusta Boulevard 773-489-0379
Hours: Mon–Fri, 8 P.M.–2 A.M.; Sat, 8 P.M.–3 A.M.;
closed Sun

Definitely one of my favorite bars. There's never a cover, a DJ spins every night, and the atmosphere and crowd are consistently laid-back and friendly. It never gets too crowded either, so you can usually find a seat or get a turn at the pool table. Owners Chuck and Laurie have been involved in the Chicago music scene for years. Chuck played in legendary Chicago punk bands The Defoliants and No Empathy, while Laurie has DJ'd at various clubs for as long as I can remember. An amusing array of punk and new wave memorabilia—from T-shirts to newspaper clippings—line the walls, and various odd toys perch behind the bar. All this and weekday drink specials as well. A must visit sort of place.

LEONA'S RESTAURANT

1936 W. Augusta Boulevard. 773-292-4300
Hours: Mon–Thu, 11 A.M.–11 P.M.; Fri–Sat, 11 A.M.–1 A.M.;
Sun, 12 P.M.–11 P.M.

For my money, Leona's has the best thin-crust pizza in Chicago. It is the standard by which I judge all other pizzas. And all other pizzas usually come up terribly short of the Leona's standard. A Chicago institution for decades, Leona's now has restaurants serving most of the city's neighborhoods. The Wicker Park location incorporates an actual brick three-flat into its facade and is a casual, convivial place to drink and fill up your guts. In addition to the pizza you can get anything from seafood dishes to burgers. The prices aren't bargains, but the portions and side dishes are large and the food is always excellent. Their specialty sandwiches deserve a mention as well—they are huge and damn tasty.

INNERTOWN PUB

 1935 W. Thomas Avenue 773-235-9795
Hours: Sun–Fri, 3 P.M.–2 A.M.; Sat, 3 P.M.–3 A.M.

The InnerTown Pub is one of my favorite Chicago bars. Though prices have gone up a bit over the years, the place still has the look and feel of a run-down Wisconsin roadhouse and you can still get domestic pints for only $2. Though Innertown is predominantly frequented by local art slobs, the clientele is fairly well mixed, with big crowds practically every night of the week. Attitude is nonexistent; it truly is a place where you can park yourself at the bar not knowing a soul and be deep in conversation only minutes later. Not that the conversation itself will always be that deep— or coherent— but, hey, at least it's friendly. The jukebox is good, and the pool tables, though not so good, are fiercely sought out each and every night. The female bartenders—and I suppose the male bartenders too—are also highly appealing to the eyes. They're not shy about pouring out a free shot or two now and then either.

DIVISION STREET

Division Street starts happening after the intersection at Ashland and Milwaukee. From here to Western you'll find a number of hipster bars and shops holding court with some old Polish bars and Mexican tire shops. After Western, Division enters Humboldt Park. You can see the large Puerto Rican flag "gateway" welcoming you to this—not surprisingly—heavily Puerto Rican neighborhood. But, unfortunately, as mentioned before, there's not a whole lot going on here to warrant anything other than a quick drive through.

ARANDAS

 1555 W. Division Street 773-252-1505
Hours: Open every day 8 A.M.–3 A.M.

Yet another Wicker Park taqueria, this one is particularly handy for late night eats. The burritos are good, and though I've always been too squeamish to try it, I'm told the menudo is quite tasty. The orchata is particularly good too.

MYOPIC BOOKS

 1726 W. Division Street 773-862-4882
Hours: Mon–Sat, 11 A.M.–1 A.M.; Sun, 11 A.M.–10 P.M.

One of the best used book stores in Wicker Park . . . or should I say one of the only used book stores in Wicker Park these days? Myopic is open nice and late, and the atmosphere here is very laid-back and comfortable, even if it is a tight squeeze between shelves. Comprised of two levels, Myopic offers a good general selection of stuff. The fiction section in particular is big and thorough. They also have plenty of art books. Not to mention a generous selection of what they delicately call "Fuck" books.

GOLD STAR

 1755 W. Division Street 773-227-8700
Hours: Sun–Fri, 4 P.M.–2 A.M.; Sat, 3 P.M.–3 A.M.

This place has been around forever, as the subdued, art-deco interior indicates. This is a very cool, low-key place to knock back a few or shoot some pool. It usually doesn't get too crowded and the prices are reasonable.

PHYLLIS' MUSICAL INN

1800 W. Division 773-486-9862
Hours: Mon–Fri, 3 P.M.–2 A.M.; Sat, 3 P.M.–3 A.M.;
Sun, 1 P.M.–2 A.M.

Another Chicago institution, Phyllis' has been in the same family since the '60s. Nothing special to look at, Phyllis' is small and comfy, with a tiny stage. Many of the bands that play here are unknown—indeed, many play their first gigs here—but the quality level is usually decent at least. If you're a hockey fan in general or a Blackhawk fan in particular, this is the place to watch games. The owner and his cohorts are fanatics. Music is featured every night. And hey, how many joints host a "Bike Messenger Night"?

LEO'S LUNCHROOM

1809 W. Division Street 773-276-6509
Hours: Sun–Thu, 8 A.M.–10 P.M.; Fri–Sat, 8 A.M.–11 P.M.

Famous throughout Wicker Park if not the rest of Chicago, Leo's Lunchroom is a funky, hopping, tiny joint serving up a great selection of mostly veggie entrées. From sandwiches and chili to more elaborate fare, the quality is always excellent. The menu changes frequently and the atmosphere is very laid back and still a bit bohemian.

D & D LIQUOR

2006 W. Division Street 773-252-3012
Hours: Sun–Thu, 9 A.M.–1 A.M.; Fri–Sat, 9 A.M.–2 A.M.

Another one of my favorite liquor stores, though not many people seem to agree with me. Okay, so the six-packs are all about a dollar more expensive here than anywhere else, but they have an outstanding selection for a neighborhood shop that makes most of its money selling malt liquor and Old Style to winos. The wine selection is also large with plenty of good deals. I very much miss the time when I lived only two short blocks from here.

THE MYSTERY SPOT

2148 W. Division Street 773-772-3364
Hours: Wed–Sat, 12 P.M.–7 P.M.; Sun, 12 P.M.–5 P.M.

 This is a fun little vintage shop. Though you won't find much in the way of clothing, there are plenty of pop culture knickknacks and toys from the '40s on up, as well as quite a bit of furniture and vintage paperbacks. There are some genuinely old items here, not just Six Million Dollar Man dolls and such. Definitely worth a visit.

BURLESQUE BOUTIQUE

2151 W. Division Street No listed phone number.
Hours: Tue–Fri, 12:30 P.M.–7 P.M.; Sat, 11:30 A.M.–5 P.M.;
closed Sun

This too is a vintage shop, and it is quite tiny. Here you'll find a small but decent selection of clothes. Most of it is fairly serviceable, run-of-the-mill sort of stuff at reasonable prices. They do have an ancient stereo and slot machine in the store as part of the decor, and if nothing else that's worth taking a look at.

NORTH AVENUE

After crossing under the Kennedy Expressway heading west, you are in Wicker Park. North Avenue has come close to replacing all the old ethnic businesses with hipster versions, but hasn't completed the task as of yet. You'll find Mexican groceries and a few bars intermingled. After Western comes Humboldt Park, which, again, isn't really worth more than a quick look-see.

QUIMBY'S QUEER STORE

1854 W. North Avenue 773-342-0910
Hours: Mon–Sat, 12 P.M.–8 P.M.; Sun, 11 A.M.–8 P.M.

Quimby's is a member of that fraternity of establishments that opened in the early days of the Wicker Park hipster settlement and developed into an institution. Though it had to move from its original digs over on Damen, the store is still one of the best of its kind. Here in its bright, spacious new location you'll find a gigantic slew of fanzines and underground comics, off-beat fiction and non-fiction, and several chapbooks and self-publications. As a matter of fact, among the stacks is one last copy of this particular writer's first novel. I told you this place is cool.

THE QUAKER GOES DEAF

 1937 W. North Avenue 773-252-9334
Hours: Mon–Thu, 11 A.M.–10 P.M.; Fri–Sat, 11 A.M.–
12 A.M.; Sun, 12 P.M.–8 P.M.

This record store may be small, but it's very appealing in layout and selection. CDs and vinyl are given equal space, and within the bins you'll find plenty of imports and rarities. They also offer a good selection of mags and 'zines.

POP ERA

 1941 W. North Avenue 773-384-4708
Hours: Mon–Sat, 11 A.M.–6:45 P.M.; Sun, 11 A.M.–4:30 P.M.

 If you're into posters, this is your place. Here you'll find a huge selection of old movie posters, band and musician posters, and various Star Trek and other pop culture subjects, plus life-sized cut-outs. And that towering cardboard replica of Xena made my blood boil—I'll tell you, by no means would I consider myself a masochist, but I must say I'd have no objections if Lucy Lawless wanted to put me in a head lock or give me a good stomping.

BORDERLINE TAP

 1958 W. North Avenue 773-278-5138
Hours: Sun–Fri, 4 P.M.–4 A.M.; Sat, 4 P.M.–5 A.M.

I have mixed feelings about Borderline. If you try to come here after the 2 A.M. bars close, good luck finding a place to stand let alone being able to wade your way up to the bar. During weekend afternoons, however, Borderline is a sunny, quiet place to kick back and down a few with friends. Of particular merit are the windows that run the length of the space. Watching people wander about the big intersection is always an enjoyable endeavor. They have some good beers on tap, too, including BBK, which always seems to make me a bit loopy.

RED DOG

1958 W. North Avenue 773-278-5138
Hours: Mon, 10 P.M.–4 A.M.; Wed, 10 P.M.–4 A.M.;
Fri–Sat, 10 P.M.–4 A.M.

If you like authentic, sweaty, high-energy dance clubs that aren't full of either suburbanites or yuppies, this is your place. Red Dog has been around for years now. Covers are typically $5 or less during the week and go up to a stiff $10 on Fridays and Saturdays. Still, if you're the type who despises all those trendy, here-today-gone-tomorrow, hyped-up monstrosities that pop up in warehouses every other week, Red Dog is worth it.

CITY SOLES

2001 W. North Avenue 773-489-2001
Hours: Mon–Sat, 11 A.M.–8 P.M.; Sun, 12 P.M.–6 P.M.

The place to buy hipster shoes in Wicker Park. This is a big, bright, comfortable shop with a wide selection for both men and women. Many of their shoes are quite expensive, but they do cut prices drastically for seasonal sales. If you can hit this store right before the change of seasons, you can clean up. Otherwise expect to pay the typical, expensive prices you'll have to pay at most places.

ESTELLE'S

2013 W. North Avenue 773-486-8760
Hours: Sun–Fri, 5 P.M.–5 A.M.; Sat, 5 P.M.–5 A.M.

Estelle's—or "It Smells" as many refer to it—is the sort of afterhours bar that you never choose to visit but somehow occasionally find yourself in anyway. Small and smoky, with a pool table taking up valuable space, Estelle's is full of sleazy shenanigans and drunken ugliness most nights. Yet even though it takes you forever to get the hardworking bartender's attention and the possibility of ever grabbing a stool is nonexistent, there is a certain charm to this place. But try not to go in there in a bad mood because you'll only make it worse. From a sociological perspective Estelle's can be interesting— especially on open mike nights during the week. Just be prepared to find yourself filled with bile and moral grime by the time you leave.

THAI LAGOON

2322 W. North Avenue 773-489-5747
Hours: Mon–Thu, 11 A.M.–10 P.M.; Fri, 11 A.M.–10:30 P.M.;
Sat, 4 P.M.–10:30 P.M.; Sun, 4 P.M.–9:30 P.M.

This attractive, sleekly designed restaurant serves up a tasty batch of traditional and "experimental" Thai dishes. As of this writing they have yet to install a bar, but that is planned for the very near future. If you like good spicy food to the accompaniment of "ambient" tunes, this is definitely a place to check out.

ARTFUL DODGER

1734 W. Wabansia Avenue 773-227-6859
Hours: Sun–Fri, 5 P.M.–2 A.M.; Sat, 8 P.M.–3 A.M.

A Bucktown institution, Artful Dodger is the place to go to dance if you're not into the club scene. Very casual and laid-back—not to mention small, dim, and colorful—this is a comfortable little joint. On Fridays and Saturdays they charge a small cover of $2.

BUCKTOWN PUB

1658 W. Cortland
Hours: Sun–Fri, 3 P.M.–2 A.M.; Sat, 3 P.M.–3 A.M.

Though the location is slightly different, the Bucktown Pub has been around since the early '70s. Low-key and comfortable, this is the ultimate neighborhood bar for both old-timers and newcomers alike. Plenty of old cartoons and artwork cover the walls, and you can drink Bucktown Lager on the cheap. Of course Bucktown Lager tastes suspiciously like Special Export, but so what? This is a cool little place to kick back and relax.

DAMEN AVENUE

Damen comes squirting up through East Village, and almost immediately after crossing Chicago Avenue begins hipsterizing itself. Though a number of ethnic businesses still exist south of Division, the same cannot be said once you're past the North/Milwaukee intersection. You are now in the heart of Bucktown, the most gentrified section of West Town, with condos, boutiques, and trendy restaurants aplenty. This goes on all the way to Fullerton.

LAVA LOUNGE

859 N. Damen Avenue 773-772-3355
Hours: Mon–Fri, 5 P.M.–2 A.M.; Sat, 5 P.M.–3 A.M.;
Sun, 6 P.M.–2 A.M.

Though Lava Lounge definitely attracts a very "stylish" crowd with DJs spinning throughout the week, it's still a small, low-key, mellow bar. From the dimly lit main area you can ascend a few stairs and kick back in a handful of rooms. The space was never changed from its origins as an apartment. Here you'll find couches, a pool table, and a pinball machine as well. Just like being at home—only here you get to be served drinks and look at attractive people.

RAINBO CLUB

1150 N. Damen Avenue 773-489-5999
Hours: Sun–Fri, 4 P.M.–2 A.M.; Sat, 4 P.M.–3 A.M.

Nelson Algren no doubt downed a few in this dark little bar—it's been around since the days of the Polish ghetto. Rather than catering to working-class stiffs, though, Rainbo has been a meeting place for Wicker Park hipsters for many years now. Wicker Park was still a bit sketchy when this conversion took place, and you'll still find a number of old timer artists about the bar now and again. I must say Rainbo always seems to bring in a large smattering of nattily dressed art gals—and guys too, I guess. Though I don't go there too often these days, back when I was young man just out of college and mistakenly engaged to be married, it was a somewhat dangerous place—practically anywhere I chose to cast a glance was a young, beautiful woman. Ah, youth. . . .

PONTIAC CAFE

1531 N. Damen Avenue 773-252-7767
Hours: Sun–Fri, 10 A.M.–2 A.M.; Sat, 10 A.M.–3 P.M.

 This place started out a few years back as a simple deli serving up vegetarian and low-fat, "healthy" items, but they've since added a bar and a huge outdoor patio for the spring and summer months. A nice place to kick back and eat some food, but don't come here expecting to eat a huge greasy burger. Live music is now offered, as well as occasional poetry readings.

ANOTHER LEVEL/LIT X

1570 N. Damen Avenue 773-252-5120
Hours: Open every day 12 P.M.–8 P.M.

 This comfortable little basement cubbyhole sells a small assortment of various "Afrocentric" items, from books and CDs to clothing and jewelry. They also sell incense and bowls—of the smoking variety, that is.

LE GARAGE

1649 N. Damen Avenue 773-278-2234
Hours: Mon, 3 P.M.–8 P.M.; Tue–Sat, 12 P.M.–8 P.M.;
Sun, 12 P.M.–6 P.M.

Specializing in designer jeans and apparel, this is the place to go if you're looking to spend an enormous wad of money. Their merchandise is, on the whole, pretty nice.

BEAT PARLOR

1653 N. Damen Avenue 773-395-2887
Hours: Mon–Sat, 12 P.M.–10 P.M.; Sun, 12 P.M.–7 P.M.

Beat Parlor offers a wide variety of house music, electronica, and hip hop—most of it on vinyl. This is a great place for DJs to stock up. They also have plenty of local releases in addition to a small number of CDs and cassettes.

DANDELION

2117 N. Damen Avenue 773-862-9333
Hours: Mon–Fri, 12 P.M.–6 P.M.; Sat, 11 A.M.–6 P.M.;
Sun, 12 P.M.–5 P.M.

Amid the many expensive, yuppie-ish boutiques along Damen, Dandelion refreshingly caters to the youthful hipster who doesn't have a disposable income comparable to the budget of a Central American nation. Though it looks very much like a boutique with its sunny interior and slick hardwood floors, you'll find standard vintage shop prices here. The selection isn't huge, but they do have three small rooms full of suit jackets, dresses, shoes, and other vintage apparel.

WESTERN AVENUE

Western begins its chug through West Town in Ukrainian Village. You'll find that Western is the least gentrified of streets in the neighborhood. But for a couple of places in Ukrainian

Village, it's the same as it was years ago, with a large number of Mexican-owned used-car dealerships and various groceries. This continues all the way to Fullerton and beyond, where the ethnic make-up of the street may change, but not its overall character.

AJAX RECORDS

1017 N. Western Avenue 773-395-4108
Hours: Tue, 1 P.M.–8 P.M.; Fri, 1 P.M.–9 P.M.; Sat, 12 P.M.–
9 P.M.; Sun, 1 P.M.–6 P.M.

A small, independent Chicago record label, Ajax is now back in the retail business once more with a new shop. In stock are many small label releases, including those from Ajax's own catalog. Don't expect to find the latest by No Doubt, but you can find bands such as Bardo Pond and Labradford. On the racks is just as much new vinyl as CDs.

EMPTY BOTTLE

1035 N. Western Avenue 773-276-3600
Hours: Open every day 3 P.M.–2 A.M.

West Town's premiere small venue for local and national acts. Drink prices are no longer dirt cheap like they used to be, but this is one of the more laid-back, independent joints in town. Bookings at Empty Bottle definitely reflect the attitude and tastes of its owner, and whether or not you get into the hipper-than-thou, art-student rock bands you're most likely to see play here, you have to admire the fact that this bar is run less for profit than as a showcase for music. During the week you'll find evenings dedicated to jazz performances as well as a "dub" night featuring DJs. Bite, the eatery within Empty Bottle, serves up "healthy" fare with a penchant for pasta dishes and vegetarian sandwiches at decent prices. They open at noon every day, and on weekends you can order from the bar at that hour as well.

LUCKY BUY/SECOND TIME AROUND

1103 N. Western Avenue 773-384-8450
Hours: Tue, 3 P.M.–7 P.M.; Wed–Thu, 11 A.M.–3 P.M.;
Fri, 3 P.M.–7 P.M.; Sat, 12 P.M.–4 P.M.; closed Sun and Mon

This cluttered little resale shop features a basic selection of clothes. And that's about it. It's nothing special, but now and then you can find some decent stuff here.

MARGIE'S CANDIES

1960 N. Western Avenue 773-384-1035
Hours: Mon–Sat, 10 A.M.–11:30 P.M.; Sun, 10 A.M.–9 P.M.

Though hopefully I'm wrong, I can't help but fear that Margie's is going to disappear soon. Located right near Arturo's and the Logan Square Village Discount, Margie's is an old time candy and ice cream fountain. Here you'll find homemade candies and chocolates as well as the best damn malts and shakes and sundaes you're ever apt to suck down your gullet.

ARTURO'S

2001 N. Western Avenue 773-772-4944
Hours: Open 24 hours

Though Lazo's next door is much bigger and less crowded, this tiny taqueria serves up better grub. This place is justifiably packed during the wee hours. Might I suggest the torta milenasa?

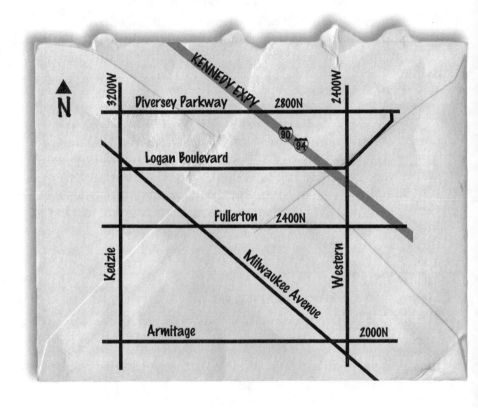

Logan Square had its heyday in the 1890s. Well-off merchants of various white ethnicities—Germans, Poles, Norwegians—built some very imposing homes along Logan Boulevard. Most of them are still standing today and function as apartment buildings. And let me tell you, these apartments are huge. I've been to a few parties in Logan Square, and I must say the apartments are among some of the nicest I've ever seen.

According to my mother, who grew up in Chicago, Logan Square was still considered a nice neighborhood through the '40s and into the '50s. That soon changed. By the early '60s the neighborhood had fallen into neglect, and Puerto Rican immigrants began moving in to take advantage of the cheap rents. Logan Square to this day remains primarily Puerto Rican. There was some trouble with gangs during the '80s and early '90s, but for the most part the neighborhood has developed into a nice place to live. Despite the number of young whites who have begun moving in, the area has retained its Latin flavor, with scores of Puerto Rican kids "cruisin'" the boulevard on weekends.

Humboldt Park to the south is also heavily

Puerto Rican these days, but it's going to take a long time before the neighborhood achieves the status of Logan Square. As of now there's a lot of poverty and not much in the way of businesses except groceries, fast food shacks, and small, used car dealerships.

VILLAGE DISCOUNT OUTLET

2032 N. Milwaukee Avenue
Hours: Mon–Fri, 9 A.M.–9 P.M.; Sat, 9 A.M.–6 P.M.;
Sun, 11 A.M.–5 P.M.

This is my favorite Village Discount. Sure its two floors are crowded and cluttered, but you can always find a decent selection of jeans and pants that—if good for nothing else—can be cut into shorts. There are also plenty of shirts and women's clothing, books, albums, and coats. The few good items take some finding among the less savory ones, but it's always worth the search.

EL YUNQUI BOOKSTORE

2556 W. Fullerton Avenue 773-235-9901
Hours: Mon–Wed, 11 A.M.–7 P.M.; Thu, 2 P.M.–7 P.M.;
Fri, 12 P.M.–7 P.M.; Sat, 10 A.M.–7 P.M.; Sun, 3 P.M.–6 P.M.

This little bookstore specializes in books by Caribbean and third world authors, including writers from Puerto Rico, Mexico, Central America, and Africa.

NEW WORLD RESOURCE CENTER

2600 W. Fullerton Avenue 773-227-4011
Hours: closed Mon; Tue–Fri, 3 A.M.–9 A.M.;
Sat–Sun, 12 A.M.–7 P.M.

This unique book shop bills itself as Chicago's only "all points of view to the left" bookstore. This is not entirely true as there are a few other such stores in the city, but I'll willingly give New World plenty of bragging rights. This is an excellent store, its large interior filled with plenty of hard to find books concerned with, well, "points of view to the left." These range from environmental and political treatises to topics such as the women's movement and labor struggles. The bargain table has some of the best 99¢ books you're ever apt to find. They also sell periodicals, CDs, and cassettes. Well worth checking out.

FIRESIDE BOWL

2646 W. Fullerton Avenue 773-486-2700
Hours: Sun–Sat, 7 P.M.–1 A.M.

Strangely enough, this small, old bowling alley has become an all-ages punk rock mecca featuring bands every night. On its small stage you can see anyone from known national acts to local suburban outfits playing their first gig—the members barely having reached puberty let alone any sort of mastery over their instruments. Not long ago the Fireside's ceiling was collapsing, the bathrooms stunk to high heaven, and the sound was absolutely terrible—yet you could still bowl at one end of the joint while bands played at the other. Now that the ceiling appears to be shored up, the bathrooms are redone, and a new sound system is in place, you can't bowl anymore. Ah well, you can still drink—if you're of age. The prices have gone up and the bartender is more likely to be shooting pool than diligently pouring suds, but so what? In only a few short years this place has become a Chicago institution. Before you know it they might even clean the tap lines.

LOGAN BEACH CAFE

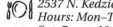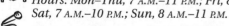

2537 N. Kedzie Boulevard 773-862-4277
Hours: Mon–Thu, 7 A.M.–11 P.M.; Fri, 8 A.M.–10 P.M.;
Sat, 7 A.M.–10 P.M.; Sun, 8 A.M.–11 P.M.

Not too many cafes bill themselves as punk rock, but the Logan Beach Cafe certainly does. Music is featured nightly, and they also cater to that civilized side all punk rockers have buried deep within

them by featuring Indonesian and Moroccan dinners on weekend nights. This is in addition to
weekend brunches. A good place to hit before the
Fireside.

Clybourn is a diagonal street running northwest through the city from Division on the south to Western on the north. However, it is generally only from Halsted to Fullerton that is referred to as the "Clybourn Corridor." This area was strictly a fading industrial strip all the way up into the '80s. Even as late as 1985, what remained outside of the few operating factories was practically a wasteland. This is hardly the case now. Since the late '80s the area has been completely turned around, sporting many monolithic "superstores," such as Home Depot, Sports Authority, and Best Buy. You'll also find plenty of upscale strip malls, expensive restaurants, and boutiques.

BLUEBIRD LOUNGE

 1637 N. Clybourn Avenue 312-642-3449
Hours: Sun–Fri, 4 P.M.–2 A.M.; Sat, 4 P.M.–
3 A.M.

Not the sort of place you'd expect to find in this strip mall part of the city. The Bluebird is dark, cozy, and "art deco," catering to a more bohemian rather than yuppie crowd. Along with a good selection of beer, they also feature Woodchuck Ale

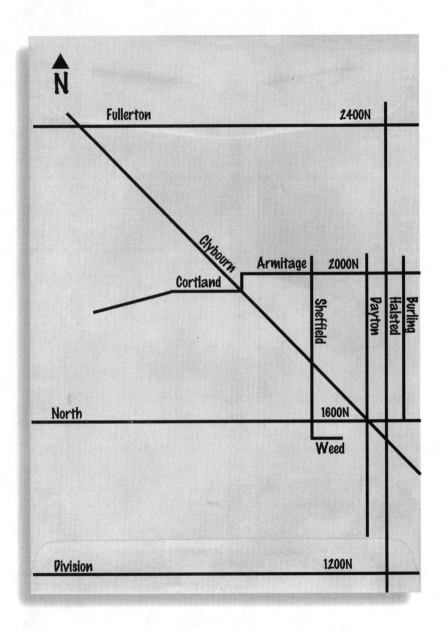

on tap—the "dark and dry" variety, which is quite tasty and satisfying. A nice place to chat and relax.

SALVATION ARMY THRIFT STORE

2270 N. Clybourn Avenue 773-477-1300
Hours: Mon–Sat, 9 A.M.–5:45 P.M.; closed Sun

With its huge parking lot, this is one of the most convenient Salvation Army stores in the city. It's also one of the biggest, with two levels. You're not likely to find too many treasures, but there's a plentiful selection of serviceable clothes and furniture.

LIAR'S CLUB

1665 W. Fullerton Avenue 773-665-1110
Hours: Sun–Fri, 8 P.M.–2 A.M.; Sat, 8 P.M.–3 A.M.

This dark little club succeeds at being both a cozy place in which to chill out and knock back a few during the off-hours and a place to get nutty on the dance floor amid the heavy crowds during the wee hours. The beer selection—though certainly not cheap—is extensive, and DJs spin throughout the week. Upstairs you'll even find a small room filled with a couple of couches and a pool table—as well as its very own bar. This is a club for people who don't particularly like clubs. The clientele is very down-to-earth and attitude is nonexistent.

WEEDS

1555 N. Dayton St. 312-943-7815
Hours: Sun–Fri, 4 P.M.–2 A.M.; Sat, 4 P.M.–3 A.M.

A Chicago institution, Weeds has occupied its small chunk of real estate for many years now. One of the more offbeat taverns in the city, Weeds is run by an enigmatic man known as Sergio Mayora: the first thing you notice upon entering is a statue of him on the bar. The crowd is laid-back and highly diverse—from tipsy senior citizens to equally tipsy young hipsters. Bands jam on the small stage and the beer garden is one of the best places to be on summer nights. A very original little suds joint.

SAM'S WINE AND LIQUORS

1720 N. Marcey Street 312-664-4394
Hours: Mon–Sat, 8 A.M.–9 P.M.; Sat, 11 A.M.–6 P.M.

Sam's has been in the neighborhood for quite some time. It used to be you could browse through its amazing stock of domestic and imported wines, beers, and liquors and then step outside and be solicited by any of the numerous prostitutes on North Avenue. The prostitutes are gone now, but Sam's—in a new building about a block away—still carries one of the best selections of alcohol in the city. If you're like me and you get excited over the prospect of sampling fine beers you've never heard of before, this is definitely a place to visit. Entering this place gets me as keyed up as going to a toy store did when I was a kid.

CROBAR

1543 N. Kingsbury Street 312-413-7000
Hours: Wed, 10 P.M.–4 A.M.; Fri, 10 P.M.–4 A.M.; Sat, 10 P.M.–5 A.M.; Sun, 10 P.M.–4 A.M.

Now that I'm an old man, it's been a long time since I've wiggled my butt on the dance floor of a "cutting-edge" nightclub. If the need were ever to arise again, Crobar would be my place of choice. The decor is very industrial and dark and the crowd, despite Crobar's longevity, is ever so trendy and hip.

EXIT

1315 W. North Avenue 773-395-2700
Hours: Sun–Fri, 8 P.M.–4 A.M.; Sat, 8 P.M.–5 A.M.

This is the same legendary institution that used to call Old Town its home. The old Exit was always an interesting place. The music leaned more toward goth and punk while the crowd ran the gamut from mohawk-sporting youths to suit-and-tie wearing yuppies. That eclecticism is a bit lost in this new location, but if you're looking for a dark, well-designed club in which to get down, this is a less "hipsterific" alternative to a place like Crobar.

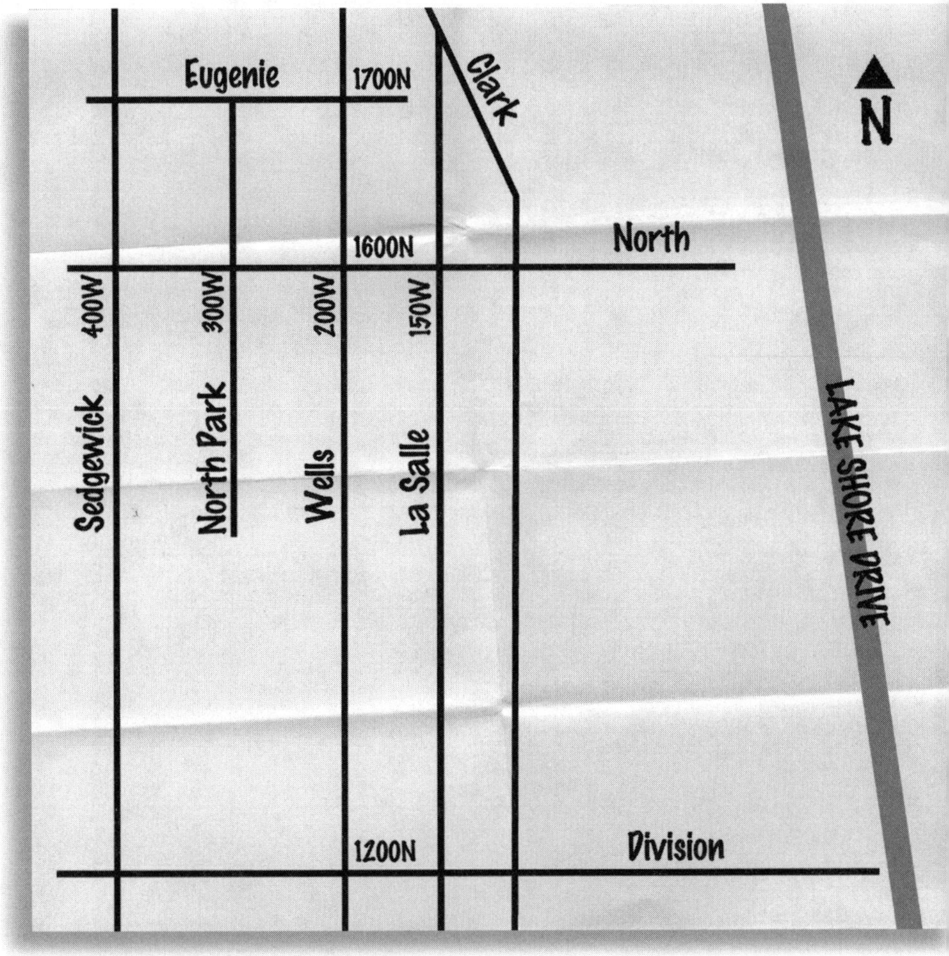
N
Eugenie
1700N
Clark
North
1600N
400W
300W
200W
150W
Sedgewick
North Park
Wells
La Salle
LAKE SHORE DRIVE
1200N
Division

O L D   T O W N

Germans originally moved here in the 1850s to escape overcrowding in their old neighborhoods, but Old Town has also played host to Hungarians and even some Italians over the years. Now it's safe to say the only real ethnic group is upper-middle-class, white American. Old Town is a very expensive place to live, and the residents are mature, professional families who have left their carefree days of yuppiedom behind. The shops are mostly expensive boutiques, and the restaurants are pricey. Not many vestiges of Old Town's '60s history remain. Back then it was a funky, artsy, "up-and-coming" neighborhood (shades of West Town), but about all you'll see of those days are a few porno shops. It was here during the '68 Democratic convention that many hippies and war protesters got their heads bashed in by the cops after nearby Lincoln Park was cleared for the night. The cops weren't satisfied with just the hippies though—they also burst into a few homes, the inhabitants of which were supposedly "taunting" the sensitive souls. Needless to say, it was "billyclubs-a-go-go" all night long.

OVER 21 BOOKSTORE

1347 N. Wells Street 312-337-8730
Hours: Open 24 hours

XXX As you can no doubt guess from the name, this is an adult bookstore. It is not particularly seedy; rather, it's the type of place some of the tipsy, well-heeled patrons of the expensive restaurants nearby might feel bold enough to enter on a lark. A typical, unspectacular selection of mags and videos are available for your perusing pleasure.

BIJOU THEATER

XXX *1349 N. Wells Street 312-943-5397*
Hours: Open 24 hours

A Chicago institution, the Bijou has been showing gay porno films for many a year now. If you're expecting some sort of seedy joint you'll be disappointed—the Bijou is actually somewhat upscale. You're not going to find a motley collection of ne'er-do-wells clandestinely stroking themselves in the dark. That's not to say, however, that there's no stroking going on. . . .

BARBARA'S BOOKSTORE

1350 N. Wells Street 312-642-5044
Hours: Mon–Sat, 9 A.M.–10 P.M.; Sun, 10 A.M.–7 P.M.

The flagship store of this small Chicago chain, Barbara's is one of the best of the independent shops featuring new books. They carry a great collection of fiction, as well as a very good selection of history, current events, and travel. Outside of the fiction section, you won't find a huge amount of books on any particular subject, but plenty of quality ones.

ADULT BOOKS

1405 N. Wells Street
Hours: Open 24 hours

XXX Unlike Over 21, this small, cramped shop is your typically seedy porno joint. In addition to video booths, you'll find many dog-eared magazines and a selection of videos—both straight and gay. This along with a small amount of "novelties" behind the counter. One of the more intriguing aspects of the place is that thrown willy-nilly under one of the bins are several old books—naughty books, you would imagine, but no, among several nondescript titles are books about Karl Marx, Saul Alinksy, and the benefits of socialism.

UP DOWN TOBACCO SHOP

1550 N. Wells Street 312-337-8025
Hours: Mon–Thu, 10 A.M.–11 P.M.; Fri–Sat, 10 A.M.–
12 A.M.; Sun, 11 A.M.-11 P.M.

This spacious, attractive store is a smoking aficionado's dream, filled to the brim with cigars, pipes, humidors, and other odds and ends.

SECOND CITY THEATRE

1616 N. Wells Street 312-337-3992
Hours: Shows Thu–Sun; call for specifics

A renowned Chicago institution, the Second City Theatre specializes in improv comedy. Take any past, current, or future Saturday Night Live cast and chances are at least half of them will be Second City alumni, from the Belushis to Chris Farley.

SEE HEAR INC.

217 W. North Avenue 312-664-6285
Hours: Mon–Sat, 10 A.M.–9 P.M.; Sun, 11 A.M.–5 P.M.

This record shop stocks a decent selection of new and used CDs. The international section is particularly strong, though all sections sport a good amount of music, not just the rock bins.

OLD TOWN ALE HOUSE

219 W. North Avenue 312-944-7020
Hours: Sun–Fri, 12 P.M.–4 A.M.; Sat,: 12 P.M.–5 A.M.

This old tavern is a bit of a Chicago institution. Within its confines you'll find plenty of social drinkers rubbing shoulders with serious barflies—quite a number of them upscale sorts with decent careers . . . at least for now. Old Town Ale House is a laid-back, low-key joint in which to get wasted. The key word here being wasted—not an activity that is generally smiled upon in most of the bars in this part of the city. Sure they'll take your money and get you wasted, but once you've achieved that goal you can pretty well bet they'll be showing you the door the second you start slurring. At Old Town you can slur as much as you want to.

LINCOLN PARK

Before the Great Fire, Lincoln Park alongside the lake was a cemetery. After the fire, the graves were removed further north and the area was turned into a park. Many German families began buying lots and building houses to the west of the park, while wealthy Anglos bought up the expensive property immediately fronting the park. This property facing the park remains very expensive and desirable to this day, and the area immediately to the west—though it had its problems up into the '60s—now enjoys the same status. In fact, by the '80s Lincoln Park was the premiere stomping ground of Chicago's yuppies. Most of these original yuppies have grown older and procreated, giving Lincoln Park—at least along Clark Street—a less festive atmosphere these days. But along Lincoln Avenue there are yuppie night spots aplenty. In fact, all of Lincoln Park is full of expensive eateries, pubs, and boutiques, but it is Lincoln Avenue between Fullerton and Sheffield that is the hot spot for partying, especially since DePaul University is in the vicinity. There are plenty of shops for every taste in the neighborhood, not to mention scads of coffee shops and bakeries and such. And if the shopping and eating

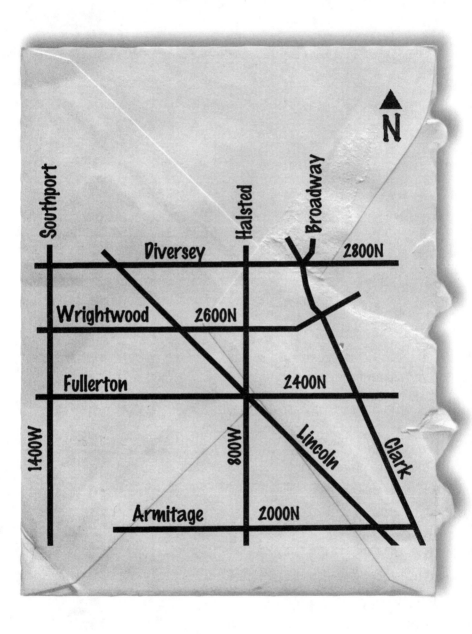

begin to lose their luster, the park and the lake are but a short walk away. Lincoln Park Zoo sets up shop here—and admission is free.

BIG JOHN'S JOINT

1147 W. Armitage Avenue 773-477-4400
Hours: Open every day 11 A.M.–2 A.M.

 This is a low-key sports bar with a mostly middle-aged crowd. What sets it apart is its food. Burgers are their specialty, but the homemade chili is damn good as well. It's also one of the few places in the city where you can get a liverwurst sandwich. I briefly worked here several years ago, and I can attest to the fact that the owner orders only the finest ingredients. And now that I'm no longer bumbling ineptly about the grill, the food's probably even better. A nice place to visit in both winter and summer, as you can either take advantage of the beer garden out back or the fireplace in the main room.

NEO

2350 N. Clark Street 773-528-2622
Hours: Sun–Thu, 10 P.M.–4 A.M.; Fri, 9 P.M.–4 A.M.;
Sat, 9 P.M.–5 A.M.

Neo's is back. A Chicago institution, it closed down for awhile but it's up and running once again. Serving the "alternative" dance crowd for well over fifteen years now, Neo's sports various theme nights during the week: "goth" night was always a popular one. And I must confess—though I was once goth myself—it was always rather amusing to see people getting down all dramatically to the bouncy, danceable beat of "Bela Lugosi's Dead." For you non-goths, I'm being sarcastic about that particular song's danceability. Imagine dancing to a Gregorian Chant and you'll get the idea.

LINCOLN PARK BOOKSHOP

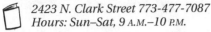

2423 N. Clark Street 773-477-7087
Hours: Sun–Sat, 9 A.M.–10 P.M.

This attractive shop features a good selection of new books—both hardcover and paperback. The travel, biography, and current events sections are particularly strong. It's the sort of bookstore that stocks solid, high-quality stuff, not the type of place in which you'll find the latest from Tom Clancy or Jackie Collins.

ZIGGY'S #1 SMOKE & NOVELTY SHOP

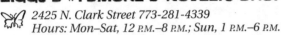

2425 N. Clark Street 773-281-4339
Hours: Mon–Sat, 12 P.M.–8 P.M.; Sun, 1 P.M.–6 P.M.

This low-key little store is the sort of place that's not supposed to exist in Chicago anymore—a head shop. The selection is very limited, but you can indeed buy bowls and bongs here. Ziggy's also sells a variety of novelty items, from postcards and patches to porno mags and vibrators. Certainly not the kind of place one is used to seeing in Lincoln Park these days.

DR. WAX

2523 N. Clark Street 773-549-3377
Hours: Mon–Sat, 11 A.M.–9 P.M.; Sun, 12 P.M.–6 P.M.

I may be overusing the phrase "Chicago institution," but Dr. Wax certainly aspires to such a designation. Now located one door down from its original digs, this new and used record store has been around for years. The CD selection is extensive and eclectic, with good showings in all categories from rock and rap to country. They also carry a small selection of new vinyl.

HI-FI RECORDS

2570 N. Clark Street 773-880-1002
Hours: Mon–Sat, 11 A.M.–8 P.M.; Sun, 12 P.M.–7 P.M.

Dealing exclusively in vinyl, Hi-Fi sports an impressive selection of new, used, and rare LPs and 45s. From lounge crooners of old to just-released Jamaican dance hall, this shop has a bit of everything.

2ND HAND TUNES

2604 N. Clark Street 773-929-6325/281-8813
Hours: Mon–Sat, 11 A.M.–8 P.M.; Sun, 12 P.M.–7 P.M.

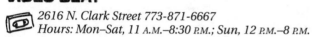 Another one of Chicago's best record stores, 2nd Hand Tunes has been a Clark Street mainstay for a long time. It is comprised of two separate stores located right next to each other. The one dealing in CDs has a decent collection of rock and international titles as well as an extensive used cassette selection. They also sell a few videos and laser discs along with a large array of posters in back. The other store is dedicated solely to vinyl. You'll find a great selection in all fields, from rock and jazz to folk and comedy.

VIDEO BEAT

2616 N. Clark Street 773-871-6667
Hours: Mon–Sat, 11 A.M.–8:30 P.M.; Sun, 12 P.M.–8 P.M.

This shop has a little bit of everything. Their specialty is music videos. All kinds of music videos, from Robert Fripp to The Cramps. Videos you thought never existed. The selection is amazing. In addition, they also have a small but decent selection of used CDs, albums, and cassettes.

GRAMAPHONE LTD.

2663 N. Clark Street 773-472-3683
Hours: Mon–Fri, 11 A.M.–9 P.M.; Sat, 10:30 A.M.–8:30 P.M.;
Sun, 12 P.M.–6 P.M.

Chicago's premiere record shop for modern dance music. Though you'll find a number of CDs, Gramaphone primarily carries vinyl for DJs. House, techno, ambient—you'll find the best selection in the city here. You can also find plenty of mix tapes from local DJs.

UNTITLED AERO

2701 N. Clark Street 773-404-9225
Hours: Mon–Thu, 11 A.M.–8:30 P.M.; Fri–Sat, 11 A.M.–
9 P.M.; Sun, 12 P.M.–7 P.M.

Clothing for the youthful skateboarding hipster. Though
the merchandise is not cheap, you can find a large collection of new shirts, tanks, and jeans here. Most of it is
oversized of course, but there's enough variety of stock
to appeal to more conservative shoppers.

DUKE OF PERTH

2913 N. Clark Street 773-477-1741
Hours: Sun–Fri, 11:30 A.M.–2 A.M.; Sat, 11:30 A.M.–3 A.M.

 This attractive, cozy bar is owned by a real live
Scotsman and features a great selection of beer, ale,
cider, and Scotch. The kitchen turns out tasty treats
like shepherd's pie and every Wednesday and Friday
you can stuff yourself silly with all-you-can-eat fish-
fries. These events are not for the claustrophobic, however, as they tend to get quite crowded. Patience is a
required virtue as well.

BOOKMAN'S CORNER

2959 N. Clark Street 773-929-8298
Hours: Open everyday 1 P.M.–6 P.M.

Bookman's Corner has been in business forever. Small
and cramped with its books piled willy-nilly amid the
shelves, it's not the most convenient of places to
search for a particular title. Yet a general browse
through the dusty stacks always manages to turn up
something interesting.

FACETS MULTIMEDIA CENTER

1517 W. Fullerton Avenue 773-281-4114
Hours: Call or check paper for screenings. Video rental
Mon–Sat, 10 A.M.–10 P.M.; Sun, 12 P.M.–10 P.M.

Facets is a combination cinema, video rental outlet,
and resource center. Its small theater features a varied

lineup of independent and foreign films throughout the week. Their video rental selection is by far the best in the city. You name it, they have it. Except for maybe twenty copies of *My Best Friend's Wedding* or *Armageddon.*

DISC GO ROUND

 2412 N. Lincoln Avenue 773-529-1133
Hours: Open every day 10 A.M.–10 P.M.

This small, new and used record shop offers a passable selection of music. CDs are not kept rigorously alphabetized. For example, any band starting with the letter *L* is simply lumped into that category in no particular order. This is rather annoying if you know what you're looking for, but if you're simply browsing, it's actually pretty cool. You end up considering quite a bit of music you otherwise might have ignored. Another plus is the fact that used CDs are always $7.99 or less, and that includes the few imports in stock as well.

LOUNGE AX

 2438 N. Lincoln Avenue 773-525-6620
Hours: Varies depending on show. Call or check paper.

A Chicago institution, Lounge Ax is one of the best small venues in which to see local and national acts. Many bands declare Lounge Ax their favorite place to play. The owners, Sue and Julia, actually treat them with respect. Live music is featured Tuesday through Saturday. You'd be advised to check local listings or call first before heading over, as Lounge Ax has been keeping an eye open for a new location for the past few years. Though things have quieted down, for a while there someone who had just moved into the neighborhood had been lodging nightly complaints. Several bands, including The Jesus Lizard, Archers of Loaf, and Seam, contributed tracks to a benefit CD to help cover the legal expenses in a dispute which, apparently, even the police found ridiculous. Lounge Ax continues to survive and thrive, however, and hopefully will continue to do so in the future.

2ND HAND TUNES

2449 N. Lincoln Avenue 773-871-1928
Hours: Mon–Sat, 12 P.M.–10 P.M.; Sun, 12 P.M.–8 P.M.

 Yet another location of the 2nd Hand Tunes juggernaut, this one distinguishes itself by offering a wide array of both mainstream and unusual videos—for sale and for rent. In addition you'll find the usual strong selection of CDs and a decent selection of albums and cassettes.

BW-3 SPORTS CAFE & PUB

2464 N. Lincoln Avenue 773-868-9453
Hours: Open every day 11 A.M.–2 A.M.

Though BW-3 is a large chain concentrated in Ohio, I feel honor-bound to mention it since within its confines they cook up the best damn wings in the city. A large bar/restaurant catering to the post-collegiate set, the place can get a bit loud during games, but they do have a take-out window in back so you don't have to spend too much time inside if you find that sort of scene off-putting. In addition to the wings, they serve up some of the best bar food anywhere—from burgers to Mexican concoctions. They also feature daily lunch specials.

ACT I BOOKSTORE

2540 N. Lincoln Avenue 773-348-6757
Hours: Mon–Wed, 10 A.M.–8 P.M.; Thu–Sun, 10 A.M.–6 P.M.

This small store specializes in drama. You'll find slews of plays here, as well as screenplays, lyrics from Broadway musicals, and books on acting, directing, and other theatrical pursuits. Also, the store encourages local playwrights to drop off scripts, which customers can read in the store.

HEALING EARTH RESOURCES and THE EARTH CAFE

 2570 N. Lincoln Avenue 773-327-8459
Hours: Mon–Sat, 10 A.M.–9 P.M.; Sun, 11 A.M.–6 P.M.

 This attractive, incense-scented shop features a wide variety of merchandise dealing with spirituality and various New Age philosophies. From books, cassettes, and videos to candles, jewelry, crystals, and greeting cards, this place has a little bit of everything—even a limited selection of clothes. Within the shop is the Earth Cafe, a small, full-service restaurant.

CLUB 950

 950 W. Wrightwood Avenue 773-929-8955
Hours: Wed–Sat, 7 P.M.–2 A.M.

One of the more enjoyable places to go if you're looking for an "alternative" dance joint. Club 950 has been up and running for years and has always been a laid-back place to hit the floor. Attitude is nonexistent here. Their '80s night, "Planet Earth," packs them in.

KINGSTON MINES

2548 N. Halsted Street 773-477-4646
Hours: Sun–Fri, 8 P.M.–4 A.M.; Sat, 8 P.M.–5 A.M.

Though this legendary club is big enough to sport two stages, the atmosphere remains very intimate, as well as loud, dark, and smoky—the perfect environment in which to see a blues band. Many famous folks have also thought so, from The Rolling Stones and The Who to Michael Jordan and various Hollywood types. The kitchen is open nightly and serves up ribs, hot wings, and catfish. Combine the latter with some good beer and blues, and you got yourself a damn good night out.

VILLAGE DISCOUNT OUTLET

2855 N. Halsted Street
Hours: Mon–Fri, 9 A.M.–9 P.M.; Sat, 9 A.M.–6 P.M.;
Sun, 11 A.M.–5 P.M.

This location is much smaller than most of the Village Discounts but does manage to remain consistent with the others in the fact that its prices are cheap, its aisles are crowded, its interior is hot and mildly stinky, and its merchandise has been picked over innumerable times. But then again, you never know. You might get lucky.

MOUNT SINAI HOSPITAL RESALE SHOP

814 W. Diversey Parkway 773-935-1434
Hours: Mon–Sat, 10 A.M.–4 P.M.; Sun, 12 P.M.–4:30 P.M.

This is sort of the Marshall Field's of resale shops. In this well-organized store you'll find plenty of high-quality merchandise. It's going to cost you, of course, but it is for a good cause.

The village of Lakeview in the mid-1800s was nothing much more than a smattering of farms and summer homes. There was plenty of room to spread out and breathe. This proved an attractive lure for a number of German families who lived in the congested neighborhood of Old Town in the 1880s. Other ethnic groups—primarily Swedes—followed their lead, and by 1920 Lakeview had close to 100,000 residents. Lakeview is still an attractive place to live, and many white, middle-class families still own homes here. Over the last decade or so plenty of white-collar professionals (along with famous resident Billy Corgan of Smashing Pumpkins) have been renting apartments or buying houses in the area too, driving up rents and property taxes so that only a remnant remains of the Mexican enclave that also used to call the area home. This is hardly surprising when you consider that within Lakeview's environs are some of the city's most popular neighborhoods like New Town (or Boys Town as it's informally known) and Wrigleyville. Lakeview covers a lot of territory, and there are plenty of "sub-neighborhoods" within its boundaries. These areas will be

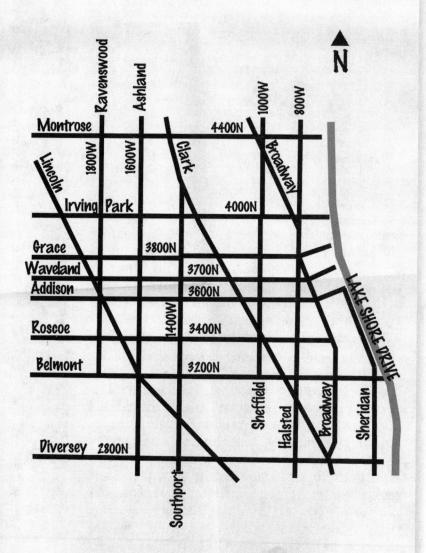

treated separately. In addition to the aforementioned Boys Town and Wrigleyville, they are the Belmont/Clark area, Southport Avenue, St. Ben, Ravenswood, Roscoe Village, and Lincoln Square. Any businesses that don't easily fit into one of these "sub-hoods" are listed below.

DELILAH'S

2771 N. Lincoln Avenue 773-472-2771
Hours: Sun–Fri, 4 P.M.–2 A.M.; Sat, 4 P.M.–3 A.M.

Old punk rockers never die, they just go to Delilah's. You won't find a high volume of yuppies here like most area bars. Delilah's caters instead to seasoned veterans of Chicago's "underground" scene. Many of the DJs who spin nightly are from legendary (or at least semi-legendary) Chicago bands, and the atmosphere is laid-back yet festive. They also have an incredible selection of beer, as well as more whiskeys than you ever imagined existed.

POWELL'S BOOKSTORE

2850 N. Lincoln Avenue 773-248-1444
Hours: Mon–Fri, 11 A.M.–9 P.M.; Sat, 10 A.M.–10 P.M.;
Sun, 11 A.M.–9 P.M.

One of three locations in Chicago, this one—as always—upholds the high Powell's standards you'll find in each of their stores. Large and spacious, Powell's carries a great, quality selection of used books on every subject. They even have a rare book room as well as bargain tables. One of the north side's best shops.

MUSKIE'S

2870 N. Lincoln Avenue 773-883-1633
Hours: Mon–Thu, 11 A.M.–10 P.M.; Fri–Sat, 11 A.M.–2 A.M.;
Sun, 11 A.M.–6 P.M.

Muskies is a classic burger joint serving up typical fast food, from burgers and hot dogs to charbroiled chicken sandwiches. Prices are cheap and the French fries aren't just tasty, they are also very liberally doled out. Though there is only a small counter and a handful of stools, in the summer they have a few small tables set up outside. A good place to dart into between bands at either the Elbo Room or Thurston's.

ELBO ROOM

 2871 N. Lincoln Avenue 773-549-5549
Hours: Sun–Fri, 7 P.M.–2 A.M.; Sat, 7 P.M.–2 A.M.

 One of Chicago's more intimate clubs in which to see local bands, Elbo Room is also one of the more attractive ones as well. The upper floor is your typical bar with pool tables, catering to a somewhat upscale crowd of . . . oh, I guess we could call them liberal yuppies. Downstairs, amid many colored candles and soft lighting, is the small stage area. You won't see many big names here, but you won't see any kids fresh out of the garage who can barely play their instruments either. During the week you'll find theme nights, from very cheap local showcases to soul and even swing bands.

THURSTON'S

 1248 W. George Street 773-472-6900
Hours: Sun–Fri, 6 P.M.–2 A.M.; Sat, 6 P.M.–3 A.M.

 Right across the street from Elbo Room, Thurston's is also a venue for local music, only many of the bands featured are of the more hard-rocking variety. Thurston's is an attractive joint as well, and is also a bit more laid-back than the Elbo Room. Surprisingly enough—for a music venue—they also serve up some tasty pasta dishes and homemade pizza. Thurston's has two levels just like Elbo Room, only here the stage is upstairs. After a few drinks you may find the spiral stairs a bit of a hazard to negotiate, so be careful.

XOINX TEA ROOM

 2933 N. Lincoln Avenue 773-665-1336
Hours: Very erratic of late. Call ahead.

Pairing an extremely sleek, attractive interior with a

very laid-back atmosphere, this is a comfortable little place to grab a cup of joe. They also feature film screenings every now and then.

WAXMAN CANDLES

 3044 N. Lincoln Avenue 773-929-3000
Hours: Mon–Wed, 11 A.M.–7 P.M.; Thu, 11 A.M.–8 P.M.;
Fri, 11 A.M.–7 P.M.; Sat, 11 A.M.–6 P.M.; Sun, 12 P.M.–5 P.M.

This candle shop is very similar in style to a Pier One. You'll find an endless variety of high quality candles and holders, with prices to match.

CHICAGO ANTIQUE CENTRE

 3045 N. Lincoln Avenue 773-929-0200
Hours: Open every day 11 A.M.–6 P.M.

This large shop features plenty of high- to mid-quality antiques, mainly from the '40s and '50s, along with plenty of '60s-era stuff as well. Prices range from very expensive to affordable. A good place to check out if you're looking for furnishings.

ARMY & NAVY SURPLUS

 3100 N. Lincoln Avenue 773-348-8930
Hours: closed Sun; Mon–Fri, 8 A.M.–5 P.M.;
Sat, 10 A.M.–5 P.M.

This is a bit of an odd store as you are not allowed to enter very far past the doorway. What you are sup-posed to do is window shop outside first, where all the merchandise is on display. The owner then goes and fetches whatever it is you wish to see. So don't take it personally if you ignore these instructions and imme-diately find yourself the center of attention. The mer-chandise is strictly military surplus, with no hip con-cessions such as jeans or blouses. The boot collection is the store's best asset.

DECIBEL RECORDS

3107 N. Lincoln Avenue 773-244-2105
Hours: Tue, 3 P.M.–8 P.M.; Thu, 3 P.M.–9 P.M.;
Sat–Sun, 11 A.M.–6 P.M.

This is a small record shop with a correspondingly small selection of merchandise. However, if you're looking for new and used hip hop and electronica CDs—not to mention old LPs—this is your place. They also have a few old rock albums.

WACKY CATS

3109 N. Lincoln Avenue 773-929-6701
Hours: Mon–Fri, 12 P.M.–7 P.M.; Sat, 12 P.M.–6 P.M.;
Sun, 12 P.M.–5 P.M.

This attractive little boutique offers high-quality, vintage clothing. For men they have mint-condition suits and tuxedos, and for women many dresses and gowns and a good selection of hats. This is the real stuff, mostly from the '50s on down. Prices are a bit high, but they reflect the quality of the merchandise.

BARGAINS UNLIMITED

3119 N. Lincoln Avenue 773-525-8595
Hours: Mon–Sat, 10 A.M.–4 P.M.; closed Sun

This small resale shop caters mostly to an elderly crowd, stocking plenty of the blouses and dresses your grandma wears as well as the pants and shirts your grandpa likes to sport. Worth a quick browse.

ARRIBA MEXICO

3140 N. Lincoln Avenue 773-281-3939
Hours: Open every day 9 A.M.–6 A.M.

This low-key Mexican taqueria serves up the tastiest chorizo burritos in the city, not to mention scads of other dishes. The dining area is large and usually hopping late at night, the jukebox blasting out your favorite Mexican ditties. And some not so Mexican. Early one evening I was dining away, along with a very small crowd. The jukebox was playing automatically, randomly selecting tunes. Imagine my surprise when a Sisters of Mercy tune came on. You just never know what the hell to expect in this world, do you?

AGATE FORCE

3341 N. Lincoln Avenue 773-529-1383
Hours: Closed Mon; Tue–Fri, 12 P.M.–7 P.M.;
Sat, 11 A.M.–5:30 P.M.; Sun, 12 P.M.–4 P.M.

This book and card shop is dedicated to popular culture—from its book and magazine titles to the novelty items about the store. The canned Spam for sale says it all. But may I just say, that stuff is a hazard. The one time I consumed some Spam I regretted it—violently— less than twenty minutes later, a land speed record for me personally. At any rate, Agate Force is an amusing little place.

ARK THRIFT SHOP

3345 N. Lincoln Avenue 773-248-1117
Hours: Mon–Thu, 10:30 A.M.–7 P.M.; Fri, 10:30 A.M.–5 P.M.;
closed Sat; Sun, 10:30 A.M.–5:30 P.M.

Ah, another mighty Ark Thrift Shop. This one has three floors and is very well-organized. Among the clothing are many serviceable items scorned by vintage store pickers such as sweatpants and sweatshirts. The furniture selection is first rate, with many reasonably priced pieces. The bargain basement is much more hit or miss. Tons of books, bicycles, mattresses, and even crutches and walkers are there to greet you.

RECORD EMPORIUM

3346 N. Paulina Street 773-248-1821
Hours: Mon–Sat, 11 A.M.–7 P.M.; Sun, 12 A.M.–6 P.M.

This comfortable, well-worn shop has a large collection of records, from Bobby Sherman to 7 Seconds to Scandal (featuring Patty Smythe, of course). But they're not for the picky. Most of the albums aren't in the best of shape, but are priced accordingly. There are plenty of CDs and cassettes, as well as a good selection of used books on music—most of them biographies of rock stars. A pleasant place to spend some time browsing.

TAI'S LOUNGE

3611 N. Ashland Avenue 773-348-8923
Hours: Sun–Fri, 7 P.M.–4 A.M.; Sat, 7 P.M.–5 A.M.

One of the more laid-back bars in Lakeview, Tai's attracts a twenty/thirtysomething clientele but that's about the only generalization you can make about the place. You'll find all sorts mingling here into the wee hours, from yuppies to hippies and everywhere in between. There are plenty of tables, a good jukebox, and lots of different beers to choose from. If you're in the area, this is one of the best 4 A.M. bars you're likely to find.

DINER GRILL

1635 W. Irving Park Road 773-248-2030
Hours: Open 24 hours

It doesn't get much more authentic than this. This is an old diner car that has been in the business of egg-and-hash slinging for many generations. The food is decent and cheap. If you're feeling brave after a night of drinking, order "The Slinger." I've experienced it once, and though it lives in my memory as exceptionally tasty, I've been too afraid to ever try it again. If I can recall correctly, it's one big platter of food consisting of—one on top of the other—two cheeseburger patties, two fried eggs, hash browns, and chili. I think that's it, though there might be a few more ingredients. Whatever the case, let's just say, don't eat this if you have any romantic plans for the next day.

BOYS TOWN

As you can probably guess from its nickname, this neighborhood is Chicago's gay capital. Gay pride flags and rainbow stickers are visible on many businesses and apartment buildings along Halsted and Broadway. Here you'll find gay bars that range in style from your typical, upscale neighborhood tavern to clubs with rather unsubtle names such as Manhole. Less concentrated than a place like the Castro in San Francisco, Boys Town has more of the flavor of another storied gay community, the Fauborg-Marigny in New Orleans—only here the population is much more yuppie in outlook and profession. Boys Town, along with its cousins in California and Louisiana, is looked upon as a respectable neighborhood, and an expensive one as well.

NANCY'S

*2930 N. Broadway Avenue 773-883-1977/
883-1616
Hours: Sun–Thu, 12 P.M.–12 A.M.; Fri–Sat,
12 P.M.–1 A.M.*

This little restaurant whips up one of the best stuffed pizzas in town. This is Chicago-style pizza for real—the slices are

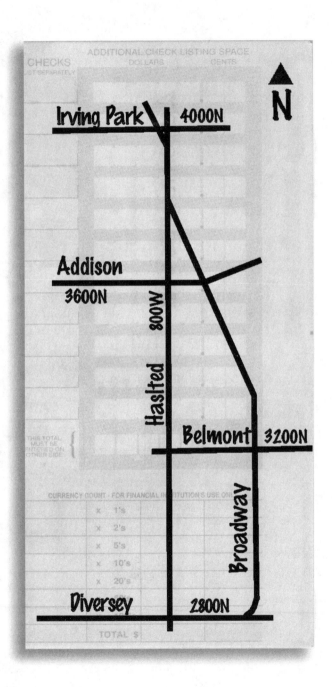

so thick and full you won't be able to down more than two pieces at most. In addition to the pizza, they also serve up a variety of sandwiches and pasta dishes—all at reasonable prices.

BOOKLEGGER'S USED BOOKS

2935 N. Broadway Avenue 773-404-8780
Hours: Sun–Thu, 11:30 A.M.–9 P.M.;
Fri–Sat, 11:30 A.M.–9:30 P.M.

Small but tidy, this place offers a decent, general selection of books as well as CDs and cassettes. The fiction section is their best asset.

BLAST OFF VIDEO

2939 N. Broadway Avenue 773-529-1650
Hours: Open every day 1 P.M.–12 A.M.

This place is for rentals only, but if you have access to a VCR over the course of your stay, definitely check it out. Though the selection isn't huge, there's some great stuff here. From Asian gangster films to Russ Meyer and '60s "girly" flicks, Blast Off carries the types of films your local video store would never think to stock.

BODY BASICS PRECISION TATTOOING AND BODY PIERCING

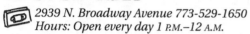

613 W. Briar Place 773-404-5669/404-5838
Hours: Mon–Thu, 12 P.M.–10 P.M.; Fri–Sat, 12 P.M.–12 A.M.;
Sun, 2 P.M.–6 P.M.

I don't have any tattoos or piercings, but I used to work at a now-defunct bookstore on Broadway where old Mad Jack, Body Basics's bearded, barrel-chested, biker-looking patriarch, would occasionally stop in. He struck me as gruff but lovable, and from what friends tell me his shop is one of the premiere tattoo parlors in the city. Mad Jack and all who work for him sport a spotless reputation for both their skill and sanitation procedures. But remember what it says on the door: "No neckties allowed." I would call first.

THE PLEASURE CHEST

XXX *3155 N. Broadway Avenue 773-525-7151*
Hours: Sun–Mon, 12 P.M.–10 P.M.; Tue–Sat, 11 A.M.–12 A.M.

A Chicago institution. This "sex boutique" caters to both gays and heteros with a small assortment of leather accoutrements, porn videos, greeting cards, and various instruments of penetration. Most formidable-looking item: "The Hand"—a life-sized, latex forearm ending in a set of steepled fingers with which you can indulge whatever whim such an item might inspire in you.

RECKLESS RECORDS

 3157 N. Broadway Avenue 773-404-5080
Hours: Mon–Sat, 10 A.M.–10 P.M.; Sun, 10 A.M.–8 P.M.

 This store is Reckless' Chicago flagship. Within its spacious interior you'll find an extensive collection of new, used, and rare CDs, vinyl, cassettes, and videos as well as fanzines and music mags. In addition they've got T-shirts and a 99-cent CD bargain bin. They also host occasional in-store appearances. Plus, if you're looking to unload any music, this is the place to come. They offer the best prices in town.

UNABRIDGED BOOKS

 3251 N. Broadway Avenue 773-883-9119
Hours: Mon–Fri, 10 A.M.–10 P.M.; Sat–Sun, 10 A.M.–8 P.M.

An attractive, independent store selling new books, Unabridged is one of the few gay-oriented book shops in Chicago. Though they stock plenty of mainstream works and have a nice children's section, their niche is definitely in gay and lesbian writers. They've got quite a large selection.

SELECTED WORKS BOOKSTORE

3510 N. Broadway Avenue 773-975-0002
Hours: Sun–Sat, 12 P.M.–9 P.M.

This cluttered, disheveled basement shop features

plenty of nooks and crannies to get lost in as you thumb through the books. The history section is the strongest, though they do have a decent selection of quality fiction. Just make sure you don't accidentally step on the cat roaming about.

NEVER MIND

3815 N. Broadway 773-975-1484
Hours: Sun–Sat, 11 A.M.–8 P.M.; closed some Sundays

I'm not sure I quite understand the name of this women's clothing store, but obviously it doesn't hurt sales any as they have another location over on Belmont. New and used dresses, blouses, and jeans are the main deal here, but they also carry an extensive selection of footwear along with handbags and other accessories.

MIKE'S BROADWAY CAFE

3805 N. Broadway 773-404-2205
Hours: Mon–Thu, 7 A.M.–10 P.M.; opens Fri, 7 A.M. and closes Sun, 10 P.M.

Mike's is not much more than a high-class Denny's (an alternative-lifestyles Denny's, you might say), but the food is substantial and good, and the atmosphere is very colorful—especially in the wee hours.

THE GALLERY BOOKSTORE

3827 N. Broadway 773-975-8200
Hours: Open every day 1 P.M.–8 P.M.

You can almost get lost in this cramped warren of shelves and nooks. The store may look chaotic, but you'll find the used stock surprisingly well-organized, with a general selection of fiction and non-fiction intermingled with many well-kept rarities. I just hope you're not claustrophobic.

LAND OF THE LOST

614 W. Belmont Avenue 773-529-4966
Hours: Closed Mon; Tue–Sat, 11 A.M.–6 P.M.;
Sun, 11 A.M.–6 P.M.

This is a nicely appointed, attractive little shop specializing in vintage clothes, games, and knickknacks. The emphasis is more on kitsch rather than high-fashion, but they do have plenty of serviceable items for the less-flashy dresser. This is in addition to a good selection of albums and old *Playboy* magazines—you may even remember a few centerfolds from your ill-spent youth. Also, the owners are good folk and the prices are generally cheaper here than in most places in the neighborhood.

ARMAGGEDON

711 W. Belmont Avenue 773-244-0666
Hours: Mon–Sat, 12 P.M.–10 P.M.; Sun, 12 P.M.–7 P.M.

Ah, I would've loved this place back in my late teens. Armaggedon is a tiny, dark record shop specializing in goth—both old and new. The selection, however, is extremely limited. CDs are the primary stock, along with a smattering of cassettes and albums. But I must say despite the slim inventory, there are a number of items here you'd be pretty hard pressed to find elsewhere.

BEATNIX

3400 N. Halsted Street 773-281-6933
Hours: Sun–Thu, 12 P.M.–9 P.M.; Fri–Sat, 12 P.M.–10 P.M.

This bright and airy used clothing shop carries plenty of tank tops, shorts, jeans, and assorted shirts for both men and women, as well as a good collection of black biker leathers. Wigs are also available, but these colorful specimens are not exactly the kind your balding great aunt would wear. In the cluttered basement you'll find more casual clothes, but the quality takes a big drop.

THE FROCK SHOP

 3402 N. Halsted Street 773-871-2728
Hours: Sun–Thu, 12 P.M.–9 P.M.; Fri–Sat, 12 P.M.–10 P.M.

Adjoining Beatnix and accessible from within that shop, The Frock Shop offers more of the same new and used clothing with more of an emphasis on (surprise, surprise) frocks and dresses.

CAFFE PERGOLESI

 3404 N. Halsted Street 773-472-8602
Hours: Unpredictable

 A Chicago institution, this place has been around for years. Small, cozy, and hippyesque, this is a nice place to down some coffee or food. Unfortunately, it seems like it's often closed. You really need to call ahead if you're going to make a special trip.

99TH FLOOR

 3406 N. Halsted Street 773-348-7781
Hours: Mon–Thu, 12 P.M.–9 P.M.; Fri–Sat, 12 P.M.–10 P.M.;
Sun, 12 P.M.–7 P.M.

Every gloomy young goth's dream—a boutique just for them! 99th Floor features Chicago's best selection of fashionable goth wear for both men and women. Their boot selection is quite impressive as well. In my younger days I forked over a decent amount of cash here.

EVIL CLOWN COMPACT DISC

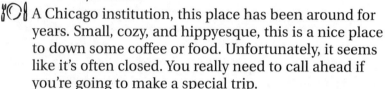 *3418 N. Halsted Street 773-472-4761*
Hours: Mon–Fri, 12 P.M.–10 P.M.; Sat, 11 A.M.–9 P.M.;
Sun, 12 P.M.–7 P.M.

As the name implies, you won't find anything but CDs here. They have a small but decent selection, both new and used. Rock is the specialty, but they do have a good selection of dance and industrial. And, oddly enough, one of the most thorough collections of Uncle Tupelo I've ever seen, God bless 'em.

CHICAGO DINER

 3411 N. Halsted Street 773-935-6696
Hours: Mon–Thu, 11 A.M.–10 P.M.; Fri–Sat, 11 A.M.–
10:30 P.M.; Sun, 10 A.M.–10 P.M.

This small, attractive restaurant features Chicago's
most extensive all-vegetarian menu. From simple
grain burgers to veggie chili, pasta dishes, and rice-
and-bean skillets, there's plenty to choose from—as
well as a choice between soy or dairy products. A good
beer selection is also available. In the spring and summer a very cozy patio is opened. Though as you know
by now I'm certainly not a vegetarian, this food is tasty
enough to make you forget meat—at least for a little
while. Though it can get a bit expensive, lunching here
on a summer afternoon on the patio is a very civilized
way to spend an hour or two.

BATTERIES NOT INCLUDED

XXX *3420 N. Halsted Street 773-935-9900*
Hours: Sun–Wed, 12 P.M.–12 A.M.; Thu–Fri, 12 P.M.–1 A.M.;
Sat, 12 P.M.–2 A.M.

This little store is one of a handful of Halsted Street sex
shops, though this one is much more properly a novelty shop. The majority of stock is comprised of nutty
little risqué gift items. They do, however, have a small
selection of the classics: vibrators, dildos, and oils.
They also advertise that 50 percent of their profits go
to charity.

WE'RE EVERYWHERE

 3434 N. Halsted Street 773-404-0590
Hours: Mon–Fri, 12 P.M.–9 P.M.; Sat–Sun, 11 A.M.–8 P.M.

A pretty traditional clothing shop, We're Everywhere
primarily features Pride T-shirts and a variety of rain-
bow-logo jackets and tanks. This in addition to jeans,
sweaters, greeting cards, keychains, and a small assortment of jewelry.

GAYMART

 3457 N. Halsted Street 773-929-4272
Hours: Sun–Wed, 11 A.M.–7 P.M.; Thu–Sat, 11 A.M.–8 P.M.

This small, nook-filled variety store is a lot of fun. It's jam-packed with everything from Star Wars memorabilia to rainbow-colored candles, clocks, T-shirts, keychains, and stationery; you can lose quite a bit of time browsing. They also sell the rather expensive but intriguing Billy and Carlos dolls. These are roughly the size of the old Hasbro G.I. Joe dolls but are action figures of the gay kind. Not only could Billy and Carlos serve as a fine companion for G.I. Joe, but—judging by their build—they could out-wrestle him in seconds flat. And Billy and Carlos are, of course, anatomically correct. No dimpled nub in the nether regions for these gentlemen.

LEATHERSPORT

 3505 N. Halsted Street 773-868-0914
Hours: Open every day 11 A.M.–1 A.M.

Billing itself as a place for "big bad boys . . . and girls," Leathersport is the kind of porn shop that makes a straight man slightly hesitant to enter. However, the shop is actually quite low-key and browser-friendly. It's the place to go for the practicing S&M aficionado. Alongside mostly gay porn videos and the usual assortment of vibrators and strap-ons and such, you'll find plenty of leather S&M apparel as well as plenty of strapping and binding devices for whatever manner of immobilization you desire.

CUPID'S TREASURE

 3519 N. Halsted Street 773-348-3884
Hours: Sun–Thu, 11 A.M.–12 A.M.; Fri–Sat, 11 A.M.–1 A.M.

This "love boutique" is the sort of high-class porn shop that gives porn shops a good name. It's the sort of place you don't feel the least bit guilty entering. Plenty of attractive couples—both hetero and gay—shop here, browsing amid the wide variety of videos, toys, and implements available. Videos are conveniently subdivided into appropriate gay/hetero/S&M/fetish categories, and there are plenty of novelty gift items available.

FLASHY TRASH

3524 N. Halsted Street 773-327-6900
Hours: Mon–Sat, 11 A.M.–9 P.M.; Sun, 12 P.M.–6 P.M.

This three-room boutique carries new and used women's clothing and accessories. Though the name of the place might lead one to think they carry plenty of polyester sundresses and such, don't be fooled. The stock, for the most part, is very fashionable, high-quality stuff: hipster tracksuits, T-shirts, shorts, sweaters, and clubwear. In back they carry a good selection of vintage dresses that actually are vintage. Prices are steep, but as mentioned, this isn't cheap, hand-me-down stuff.

BROWN ELEPHANT RESALE SHOP

3651 N. Halsted Street 773-549-5943
Hours: Open every day 11 A.M.–6 P.M.

This huge, warehouse-size resale shop prominently displays Pride flags throughout its interior. And let me tell you—the gay community knows how to run a resale shop. This is the best you're going to find in the city, with proceeds benefiting the Howard Brown Health Center (for AIDS and HIV patients). Vintage-shop-quality stuff for resale shop prices can be found among the lengthy aisles here, from sweatshirts and jeans to footwear and furnishings. The albums are all priced $1 and are even alphabetized. As for the books, the set-up rivals some bookstores I've seen. They even sell CDs.

JAVA JOE'S

3700 N. Halsted Street 773-528-3700
Hours: Mon–Thu, 10 A.M.–11 P.M.; Fri–Sat, 10 A.M.–
12 A.M.; Sun, 10 A.M.–8 P.M.

This comfortable coffeehouse features acoustic performances—jazz, blues, country, and bluegrass. The
kitchen is open late and the menu is extensive. They
also serve ice cream.

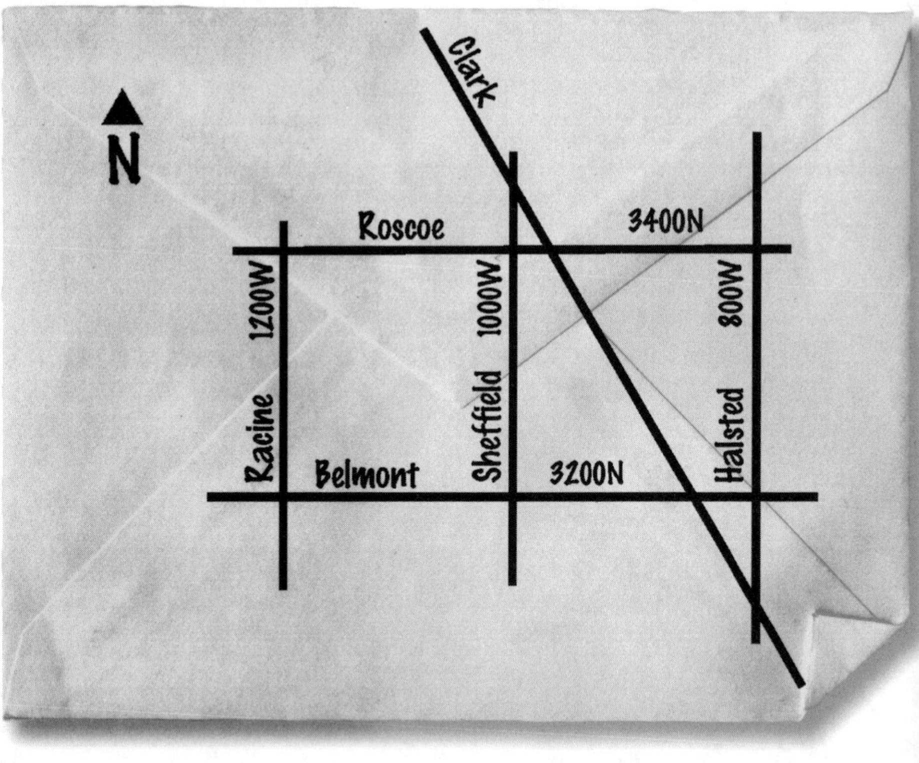
N
Clark
Roscoe
3400N
1200W
1000W
800W
Racine
Sheffield
Halsted
Belmont
3200N

BELMONT AND CLARK

Before Chicago's Swedish community thoroughly established themselves in Andersonville around the turn of the century, a number of Swedish families settled in the Belmont/Clark area. Here they could converse in their native tongue and find out about lodging and jobs. Though a hundred years have gone by, the Belmont/Clark area still acts as a magnet, only now it draws teenage suburban hipsters. Back when I was a tender youth of seventeen—and, admittedly, something of a suburban hipster— this was the happening place to be. You would drive straight into the neighborhood from your outlying suburban burg of origin, find a place to park, and then engage in some serious hanging out—or, as the authorities called it, loitering. The legendary juice bar that was the beacon about which we radiated—Club Medusa—is long gone now, but the number of hipster shops catering to the disaffected youth of today has shot through the roof. Indeed, this is the premiere "alternative" shopping district in the city. And yes, it is somewhat comforting to still see mohawk-sporting youngsters and skinheads fashionably begging change outside the "Punkin' Donuts" just as they did in my youth. Of course they are joined now by hordes of scrawny teenagers in clothes many times too big for them or decked-out like funky little goateed Greg Bradys, but, overall, nothing has changed. If anything, the area is more popular than ever.

SOLE JUNKIES

 3176 N. Clark Street & 913 W. Belmont Avenue
773-529-1944/348-8935
Hours: Mon–Sat, 11 A.M.–8 P.M.; Sun, 12 P.M.–6 P.M.

If you're looking for unique, brand-new hipster footwear—and are willing to fork out a lot of cash—this is the place to go. The two locations are practically right around the corner from each other. Here you'll find a wide selection of chunky-heeled boots and shoes and various hep, brand-name sneakers.

ROCKET 69

 3180 N. Clark Street 773-472-7878
Hours: Mon–Sat, 10 A.M.–10 P.M.; Sun, 11 A.M.–8 P.M.

This little combination head shop/hipster boutique has been around many years now. Inside you'll find a few bongs and bowls along with "alternative" greeting cards, candles, and incense, and various Hindu stat-uettes and the like. Back in the old days we suburban gadabouts always made sure to include this place on our evening's itinerary. We were damn glad to have it too. Unlike you spoiled youngsters, we didn't have an endless succession of cool shops to visit. And I can still remember those little bottles of Liquid Rush we used to purchase here—we didn't even know you're supposed to use that stuff for sex. Instead we simply took a sniff or two every now and then and watched the streetlights swim and buzz and felt the momentary "catharsis" of what we called the Death Buzz. Ah, yes, the pleasures of youth. . . .

DISC GO ROUND

3182 N. Clark Street 773-404-4955
Hours: Mon–Sat, 10 A.M.–10 P.M.; Sun, 12 P.M.–7 P.M.

This small, new-and-used music shop is indeed a cousin of the one in Lincoln Park. It too offers a passable selection of music. CDs are not kept rigorously alphabetized; any band starting with the letter *L* is simply dumped into that category in no particular order. As I mentioned before, this is rather annoying if you know what you're looking for, but if you're simply browsing, you end up considering quite a bit of music you otherwise might have ignored. Another plus is the fact that used CDs are always $7.99 or less, even the few imports.

GOSO-LO

3212 N. Clark Street 773-529-2681
Hours: Mon–Fri, 11 A.M.–7 P.M.; Sat, 11 A.M.–5 P.M.;
Sun, 12 P.M.–5 P.M.

This two-level shop features new clothing upstairs for the young female hipster as well as a few shirts for men. In the basement it's bargains galore. Everything is used, and nothing sells for more than $20. They have plenty of footwear, suit jackets, and tie-dyed T-shirts.

MAMA DESTA'S RED SEA ETHIOPIAN RESTAURANT

3218 N. Clark Street 773-935-7561
Hours: Mon, 4 P.M.–10:30 P.M.; Tue–Thu, 3 P.M.–10:30 P.M.;
Fri–Sun, 11:30 A.M.–11:30 P.M.

As the name tells you, this place serves up Ethiopian food, which I'd never had until eating here a few years back. I must say I was impressed. Whether you're a vegetarian or a voracious carnivore such as myself, Mama Desta's gives you heaping platefuls of both meat and vegetable dishes at reasonable prices. And yes, they do have African beer.

TWO DOORS SOUTH

 3230 N. Clark Street 773-404-7072
Hours: Open every day 12 P.M.–8:30 P.M.

Ah, a place for the inner hippie in all of us. In this tiny little shop you'll find plenty of trippy-dippy jewelry, incense, and candles.

SMUGGLER'S ROW

3238 N. Clark Street 773-528-0885
Hours: Open every day 12 P.M.–8 P.M.

 After visiting Two Doors South and getting in touch with your inner hippie, you might decide to indulge him or her a little at Smuggler's Row. In this dark, inviting den, you can find a variety of tie-dyed dresses, shirts and pants, and handmade shawls and pouches. They also carry sunglasses and the obligatory incense and jewelry. Some nicely crafted bowls are also available. Bowls for smoking, that is, not ones in which to eat lentil soup.

THE DOC STORE

3240 N. Clark Street 773-244-0099
Hours: Mon–Sat, 12 P.M.–8 P.M.; Sun, 12 P.M.–6 P.M.

A Dr. Marten aficionado's dream. This small shop offers a wide selection of the Doctor's finest footwear, not to mention an extensive collection of patches and stickers. Sunglasses, T-shirts, and jewelry are also available.

SHIROI HANA RESTAURANT

3242 N. Clark Street 773-477-1652
Hours: Mon–Thu, 12 P.M.–2:25 P.M. and 5 P.M.–9:55 P.M.;
Fri–Sat, 5 P.M.–10:25 P.M.; Sun, 4:30 P.M.–9:25 P.M.

This bustling little Japanese restaurant serves up a fine selection of fare, from sushi and your basic teriyaki and tempura dishes to a wide variety of seafood. Prices aren't cheap but they are reasonable and the food is worth it. Another plus is the variety of Japanese beers available. Of course in my limited experience I've found that all Japanese beer tastes the same, but still, in my book, the more beer selections available, the better the restaurant.

CHICAGO COMICS

 3244 N. Clark Street 773-528 -1983
Hours: Mon–Fri, 12 P.M.–8 P.M.; Sat, 11 A.M.–8 P.M.;
Sun, 12 P.M.–6 P.M.

Here in this spacious shop you'll find a good collection of small press, import, and adult comics as well as a small bin of back issues—mostly of the superhero ilk. But I have to ask, who buys adult comics? I mean it seems like some of them might be interesting—not to mention "titillating" but would you be more embarrassed to buy an X-rated comic or a Hustler? Is buying the comic a cop out, or is it a sign of intellectualism? Hmm . . . anyway, they also carry a number of model kits as well as several offbeat nonfiction books.

CHICAGO MUSIC EXCHANGE

 3264 N. Clark Street 773-477-0830
Hours: Mon–Fri, 11 A.M.–7 P.M.; Sat, 12 P.M.–6 P.M.;
Sun, 12 P.M.–5 P.M.

Within the small confines of this place you'll find a great selection of used and vintage guitars and amps. They also do repair work, and are quite nice about it. A friend of mine once brought a guitar in for some work, went out of town, and completely forgot about it. When he returned two months later had they sold it? No. Had they smashed it to bits? No. Did they even charge him a storage fee? No. Noble folks, I tell ya.

MEDUSA'S CIRCLE

3268 N. Clark Street 773-935-5950
Hours: Tue–Sat, 12 P.M.–8 P.M.; Sun, 12 P.M.–6 P.M.

The place to go for the young femme fatale goth. This boutique features new, used, and vintage clothing for the doom-and-gloom set. Plenty of black—both in clothes and makeup—to choose from.

DISGRACELAND

3330-A N. Clark Street 773-281-5875
Hours: Mon–Sat, 11 A.M.–7 P.M.; Sun, 12 P.M.–6 P.M.

This new-and-used women's clothing shop doesn't specialize in vintage so much as just plain old modern hipster wear. They carry a decent selection of stuff, including a few men's T-shirts and jeans. They also pay cash for used clothes, so if you're looking to part with any threads, give them a visit.

HUBBA-HUBBA

3338 N. Clark Street 773-477-1414
Hours: Mon–Sat, 11 A.M.–7 P.M.; Sun, 12 P.M.–5 P.M.

This is a vintage store that lives up to its name. You'll find many items from the '30s and '40s here, most of it for women and most of it expensive. The stock is very elegant and high quality, so paying high prices for this merchandise is not like spending a ridiculous amount of money on an Adidas sweatshirt from the seventies. In fact, back one Christmas in the days when I was just out of college and poor(er), I bought my girlfriend an expensive, full-length skirt from here. It was from the '30s and quite elegant. Of course we broke up only a few weeks later so I never got to see her wear it, but that's beside the point. Do I regret having tossed all that money Hubba-Hubba's way? Of course not. Did I ever weep over how many cases of Black Label I could have bought with that money? Of course not. Never. Not once. . . .

HOLLYWOOD MIRROR

812 W. Belmont Avenue 773-404-4510
Hours: Mon–Thu, 11 A.M.–8 P.M.; Fri–Sat, 11 A.M.–9 P.M.;
Sun, 11 A.M.–7 P.M.

Walking into this large, colorful, sunny retro shop kind of makes you feel like you're entering a kaleidoscope. Or at least it made me feel that way once. Of course that could have been due to the contrast between the heat outside and the air-conditioning inside and the resulting head rush I experienced, but whatever the case, you'll find this quite an attractive store. They carry a large selection of jeans, shirts, toys, and lava lamps along with dresses and footwear. In the basement you'll find more clothes as well as vintage kitchen tables straight from the '50s and '60s. Unfortunately, prices are a bit steep, but the merchandise is of good quality. Don't tell them I gave you this advice, but even if you're not up to dropping any dough, this place is still worth visiting.

RAGSTOCK

812 W. Belmont Avenue (upstairs) 773-868-9263
Hours: Mon–Thu, 10 A.M.–9 P.M.; Fri–Sat, 10 A.M.–10 P.M.;
Sun, 12 P.M.–7 P.M.

This large, spacious shop above Hollywood Mirror is a favorite with the kids, both male and female. Amid the racks are many new and used dresses, tank tops, jeans, T-shirts and footwear—along with an extensive selection of camouflage pants. Most of the stock is fairly expensive, yet here and there are many good deals—such as new T-shirts for only $3.50. They might not survive more than two washes, but hey, what do you expect at that price?

PHILLY'S BEST

855 W. Belmont Avenue 773-525-7900
Hours: Mon–Thu, 11 A.M.–12 A.M.; Fri–Sat, 11 A.M.–2 A.M.;
Sun, 12 P.M.–9 P.M.

This fast food joint bills itself as the best place outside Philadelphia to get cheese steak sandwiches. Unfortunately I haven't yet been to Philadelphia, but if that city regularly churns out tastier cheese steaks than Philly's Best, I might just have to move there. Their other sandwiches—which are baked and called "oven grinders"—are huge and tasty as well. They also serve pizza and salads. Not exactly cheap, but you definitely get more than your money's worth.

PINK FROG

857 W. Belmont Avenue 773-525-2680
Hours: Mon–Sat, 11 A.M.–7:30 P.M.; Sun, 1 P.M.–6 P.M.

This girly shop deals in new clothing and footwear. Much of it is quite hip and could come in handy for clubbing and such, but they do have more mundane offerings for the corporate environment as well. The prices aren't bad either—not as high as you would expect.

THE ALLEY a.k.a. THE ALTERNATIVE SHOPPING COMPLEX

858 W. Belmont Avenue 773-883-1800
Hours: Mon–Thu, 10 A.M.–10 P.M.; Fri–Sat, 10 A.M.–12 P.M.;
Sun, 12 P.M.–8 P.M.

Historians like to compare the modern shopping mall to Medieval cathedrals in terms of the social impact they have on the surrounding community. Much like the dirt-floored shack of a church that eventually metamorphosed into a spectacular cathedral, so too has The Alley grown from its humble origins as a small, cluttered head shop on Broadway. It is now a mini-mall of its own, and like the cathedrals of old, it weekly draws hundreds of dedicated, youthful pilgrims from the city and suburbs, who quiver in fits of materialistic ecstasy once they enter. Here amid various interconnected shops you will find everything from gothic clubwear to T-shirts, jewelry, footwear, leather jackets, swords (yes, swords), plaster columns and gargoyles, cigars and humidors, and even lingerie, condoms, and vibrators. None of it is particularly cheap, but even if you're not looking to buy anything, The Alley is definitely worth a visit.

EGOR'S DUNGEON

 900 W. Belmont Avenue 773-525-7131
Hours: Mon–Thu, 12 P.M.–10:30 P.M.; Fri–Sat, 12 P.M.–
12 A.M.; Sun, 12 P.M.–10 P.M.

 This small shop is a combination head shop/porn
shop. The selection is fairly limited, but they do have a
nice collection of bowls. A few whips, some items of
lingerie and a smattering of porno videos and vibrators flesh things out, so to speak.

THE CHICAGO TATTOOING COMPANY

 922 W. Belmont Avenue 773-528-6969
Hours: Mon–Sat, 12 P.M.–12 A.M.; Sun, 2 P.M.–12 A.M.

This place bills itself as one of Chicago's oldest tattoo
parlors—and one of the best. A friend of mine has gotten a tattoo here and was quite pleased with the crafts-
manship and the procedure, and I have no reason to
disagree. Keep in mind, however, that they don't even
want to see you walking through the door unless
you're eighteen.

RECORD EXCHANGE

 925 W. Belmont Avenue 773-975-9285
Hours: Mon–Sat, 11 A.M.–10 P.M.; Sun, 11 A.M.–6 P.M.

In this comfortable, laid-back shop you'll find a decent
selection of both new and used CDs as well as an
extensive selection of cassettes and vinyl. As for the
vinyl, we're not just talking about '70s rock. They carry
a prodigious amount of jazz, blues, country, and even
classical.

TRAGICALLY HIP

 931 W. Belmont Avenue 773-549-1500
Hours: Mon–Tue, 11 A.M.–7 P.M.; Wed–Thu, 11 A.M.–8 P.M.;
Fri–Sat, 11 A.M.–7 P.M.; Sun, 11 A.M.–6 P.M.

Yep, the name says it all. This is, indeed, a retro clothing store. Bet you couldn't have guessed. Catering
mostly to women, this place stocks conventional,

expensive stuff. The place to go if you want stylish, hip clothing that can be worn at the office.

BELMONT ARMY SURPLUS

 945 W. Belmont Avenue 773-975-0626
Hours: Mon–Sat, 11 A.M.–8 P.M.; Sun, 1 P.M.–6 P.M.

 This place has come a long way from the days when the clerks used to reprimand you for poking through a stack of jeans. In fact, upon entering, you might decide that the sign out front is misleading. The first floor is given over entirely to pricey, brand-new hipster wear—both clothing and footwear. Upstairs, however, you'll find a wide variety of army surplus gear as well as an extensive collection of leather jackets. And the clerks, I might add, are now friendly.

NEVER MIND

 953 W. Belmont Avenue 773-472-4922
Hours: Mon–Sat, 11 A.M.–8 P.M.; Sun, 12 P.M.–6 P.M.

 Kind of an odd name for a women's clothing store, don't you think? Anyway, within its confines you'll find a wide variety of affordable dresses, blouses and shirts, and footwear. These range in style from the near-conservative to hoity-toity club wear. Strangely enough, I've even found a couple of dirt-cheap, brand new pairs of men's long underwear pants here. Happy hunting.

BERLIN

 954 W. Belmont Avenue 773-348-4975
Hours: Sun–Fri, 5 P.M.–4 A.M.; Sat, 5 P.M.–5 A.M.

The Berlin nightclub has been a Chicago institution for many years and is one of the city's best known lesbian bars—though, of course, they advertise that they cater to "every sexuality." And indeed, they even have a "Boys' Night." Dark and smoky inside, Berlin is the place to go if you're looking to wiggle about on a dance floor.

MUSKIE'S

 963 W. Belmont Avenue 773-477-1880
Hours: Mon–Thu, 6 A.M.–2 A.M.; Fri–Sat, 6 A.M.–4 A.M.;
Sun, 6 A.M.–12 A.M.

Muskie's is one of the better traditional fast food joints
in town, with a wide range of items to pick from
including burgers, gyros, and hot wings. What really
sets it apart, though, are the number of vegetarian
entrées on the menu. The fries are damn good, too.
They're of the skinny variety, the kind you can pop into
your mouth ten at a time.

LEONA'S RESTAURANT

 3215 N. Sheffield Avenue 773-327-8861
Hours: Sun–Thu, 11 A.M.–12 A.M.; Fri–Sat, 11 A.M.–
1:30 A.M.

This is the restaurant that started it all. From here the
Leona's empire was able to expand throughout the city.
As I've mentioned before and as you'll no doubt read
again in upcoming pages, for my money Leona's
makes the best damn thin-crust pizza in Chicago—if
not the world. The rest of the menu is no slouch either,
from huge specialty sandwiches to pasta and seafood
dishes. As for the restaurant itself, your dining experience will be casual, fun, and—considering this is one
of their busier locations— loud and somewhat
crowded as well. But all the same, I'm sure you'll find
the food very much worth it.

SHEFFIELD'S WINE AND BEER GARDEN

 3258 N. Sheffield Avenue 773-281-4989
Hours: Mon–Thu, 3 P.M.–2 A.M.; Fri, 2 P.M.–2 A.M.;
Sat, 12 P.M.–3 A.M.; Sun, 12 P.M.–2 A.M.

A place like Sheffield's is very hard to find in this
neighborhood. Though it regularly gets quite crowded
and loud, the bar always retains a low-key, relaxed
atmosphere. The patrons tend to be a bit more "artsy"
than the crowds you'll find at most area bars, and the
place even sports a back room where small drama pro-

ductions are occasionally staged. More pluses: dozens of beers, paintings by local artists, and one of the most attractive beer gardens in town—they even have a pool table set up in it. The most unusual attraction here, however, is the enormously fat cat that roams the top of the bar at will, casually winding his way amid the glasses and bottles to his water bowl at the far end—a gigantic martini glass. Then again, considering how fat he is and how often you'll find him lapping away, that glass just might not be filled with water.

THE STARS OUR DESTINATION

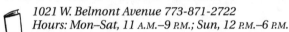

1021 W. Belmont Avenue 773-871-2722
Hours: Mon–Sat, 11 A.M.–9 P.M.; Sun, 12 P.M.–6 P.M.

This is something you don't see very often—at least not in Chicago: a bookstore devoted entirely to sci-fi, fantasy, and horror. There's a large collection here in both hardcover and paperback—both new and used. In addition you'll find related magazines, Star Trek memorabilia, and T-shirts. I find this a particularly nice place to browse as it takes me back to my geeky, early high school days when all I read was sci-fi and fantasy. (I wanted to grow up to be like Conan the Barbarian, don't you know.) If these genres are your cup of tea or you simply feel like getting nostalgic, this is definitely a place to visit.

MOTI MAHAL INDIAN RESTAURANT

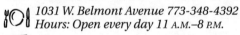

1031 W. Belmont Avenue 773-348-4392
Hours: Open every day 11 A.M.–8 P.M.

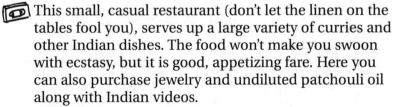 This small, casual restaurant (don't let the linen on the tables fool you), serves up a large variety of curries and other Indian dishes. The food won't make you swoon with ecstasy, but it is good, appetizing fare. Here you can also purchase jewelry and undiluted patchouli oil along with Indian videos.

SOMETHING OLD SOMETHING NEW

1056 W. Belmont Avenue 773-271-1300
Hours: Mon–Fri, 9 A.M.–9 P.M.; Sat–Sun, 9 A.M.–8 P.M.

This huge shop carries both used and new clothing at very reasonable prices. They have plenty of jeans, shirts, dresses—you name it. You probably won't find any big name brands or exceedingly funky apparel, but for your average, no-nonsense clothing, this place is perfect.

WHY NOT CAFE

1059 W. Belmont Avenue 773-404-2800
Hours: Mon–Thu, 9 A.M.–1 A.M.; Fri–Sat, 9 A.M.–2 A.M.;
Sun, 10 A.M.–12 A.M.

Comfortable and quiet, the Why Not Cafe does something that most coffee houses do not: They serve up a good selection of omelettes. This is in addition to the more traditional sandwiches and salads along with all the joe. They also offer a decent selection of used books for sale.

FUNKY TOWN

1123 W. Belmont Avenue 773-665-1803
Hours: Mon–Thu, 1 P.M.–8 P.M.; Fri, 1 P.M.–9 P.M.;
Sat, 12 P.M.–9 P.M.; Sun, 12 P.M.–6 P.M.

I must say that out of all the retro clothing stores in the neighborhood, this one has not only the most retro feel, but the most colorful interior and merchandise as well. Along with jewelry and footwear, you'll find plenty of zany polyester shirts, flower-print dresses, and bell-bottoms. By the time you leave you'll be itching to make love not war.

DESERT TREAT

1125 W. Belmont Avenue 773-871-1696
Hours: Mon–Sat, 11 A.M.–10 P.M.; Sun, 12 P.M.–9 P.M.

This small, low-key Middle-Eastern restaurant doesn't have an extensive menu or serve up anything that will knock you off your feet, but the food is good, the portions are decent, and the prices are reasonable. What would I recommend? The falafels, and thank you for asking.

WRIGLEYVILLE

Still a somewhat sketchy neighborhood only fifteen years ago, Wrigleyville is now one of the more popular neighborhoods in the city. The home of the Cubs, Wrigley Field, is the main draw, of course, but there are plenty of bars, clubs, restaurants, and shops dotting the area to keep people busy in the off-season, including quite a few Japanese eateries. The blue-collar whites who once owned homes in the area have been replaced by the ubiquitous white professionals and their large dogs. For most city dwellers, Wrigleyville long-ago replaced Rush and Division as the city's premiere party destination, and on nights after Cubs games, an almost Bourbon Street/Animal House atmosphere pervades the neighborhood.

PICK ME UP CAFE

 3408 N. Clark Street 773-248-6613
Hours: Mon–Thu, 5 P.M.–5 A.M.; Opens Fri, 5 P.M.
and closes Sun, 5 A.M.

A great place for those who like to brace themselves late at night with some coffee, this colorful, comfortable cafe serves up

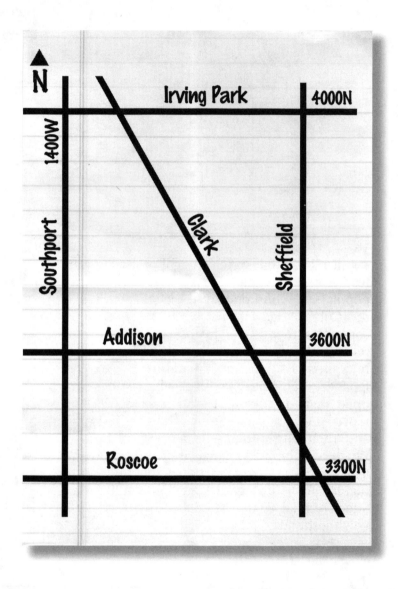

food and joe throughout the wee hours. A good place
to stop on the way home after drinking if you can feel
a hangover looming in your immediate future.

REVOLUTION BOOKS

3449 N. Sheffield Avenue 773-528-5353
Hours: Wed–Fri, 3 P.M.–8 P.M.; Sat, 12 P.M.–6 P.M.;
Sun, 12 P.M.–4 P.M.

What every city needs, its own leftist, agit-prop book shop. This basement store features plenty of works on the wonders of socialism and the evils of corporate capitalism. A fine place to gift shop for that know-it-all right-winger in the family.

THE BOOKWORKS

3444 N. Clark Street 773-871-5318
Hours: Mon–Thu, 12 P.M.–10 P.M.; Fri–Sat, 12 P.M.–11 P.M.;
Sun, 12 P.M.–6 P.M.

This is one of my favorite used bookstores, but then I'm a bit partial to this joint since I used to work here many years ago. The owners, Bob and Ronda, are good people and the overall selection is great—especially the fiction and art sections. They also have plenty of albums, CDs, and some cassettes. In addition to all the used stuff, you'll also find an extensive selection of new books by Kerouac, Bukowski, and Burroughs.

STRANGE CARGO

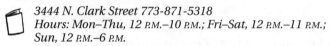

3448 N. Clark Street 773-327-8090
Hours: Mon, 12 P.M.–6:30; Tue–Fri, 12 P.M.–6:45 P.M.;
Sat, 11 A.M.–6:45 P.M.; Sun, 12 P.M.–5:30 P.M.

This sunny, good-sized shop has a decent stock of typical vintage shop clothes for men and women as well as an extensive selection of leathers, shoes, and jeans. And plenty of fedoras—the perfect accessory for any well-dressed man or woman.

FLASHBACK COLLECTIBLES

3450 N. Clark Street 773-929-5060
Hours: Mon–Sat, 12 P.M.–7 P.M.; Sun, 12 P.M.–5 P.M.

Stepping into this place is like being back in a dime store as a kid. There's plenty of old junk to keep you flitting about the shop. From board games to patches and cheap little toys, you'll find plenty to remind you of what it was like to be a young kid in the '70s. Plus, if you had pin-up photos in your room—you know, those soft-focused, feathered-haired shots of Andy Gibb and Farrah Fawcett—you'll be able to restock your collection.

BACK-A-YARD RESTAURANT

3474 N. Clark Street 773-281-5224
Hours: Sun–Fri, 5:30 P.M.–2 A.M.; Sat, 5:30 P.M.–3 A.M.

This funky little Jamaican restaurant serves up a great selection of fare, from curries and jerk chicken to saltfish. A great place to knock back some food either before or after hitting the Wild Hare.

WRIGLEY FIELD

1060 W. Addison Street 773-404-2827
Hours: Varies depending on game time. Check paper or call.

Need I even mention that this place is a Chicago Institution? One of the better-known historical stadiums in the country, Wrigley Field is a pleasant place to pass an afternoon or evening. The bleachers cost $12 usually, and only $6 on certain days, but the entertainment value of the "bleacher bums" about you is priceless. After the Cubs' "sort of" playoff appearance at the end of the '98 season and Sammy Sosa's monster home-run stretch, attendance will no doubt be heightened for at least a couple of years. Therefore don't expect the solitude most hardcore Cub fans have traditionally enjoyed during weekday afternoons. Yet unlike the horrific, mall-like travesty that is the new Comiskey Park in Bridgeport where the Sox play, Wrigley Field is full of personality and crazy fans. If you're here in spring or summer, taking in a game is well worth it.

YESTERDAY

1143 W. Addison Street 773-248-8087
Hours: Mon–Sat, 1 P.M.–7 P.M.; Sun, 2 P.M.–6 P.M.

This weathered, tattered place carries just the sort of merchandise you'd expect from its facade. Inside you'll find plenty of old, tattered *Life* magazines, posters, paperbacks, comics, and an extensive collection of sports cards. They even have an O. J. Simpson card. How strange, that whole O. J. Simpson deal. When I was a kid, he was the guy I most wanted to emulate. Of course, being white and losing whatever speed I had by the age of twelve made this hopeless. Still though, that's kind of the story of my life: My boyhood hero turns out to be a double-murdering creep.

THE WILD HARE & SINGING ARMADILLO FROG SANCTUARY

3530 N. Clark Street 773-327-4273
Hours: Sun–Fri, 8 P.M.–2 A.M.; Sat, 8 P.M.–3 A.M.

A Chicago institution—yes there are many of them in Wrigleyville—The Wild Hare is Chicago's premiere, long-enduring reggae club. Live music is featured every night but Monday, with local, national, and even occasional Jamaican acts. In the summer this place gets crowded and hot—not to mention smoky. A great place—and there's no cover before 9:30.

JIMMY AND TAI'S WRIGLEYVILLE TAP

3724 N. Clark Street 773-528-4422
Hours: Open every day 3 P.M.–2 A.M.

Though I primarily look upon the Wrigleyville Tap as the place to swig down beers before catching a band next door at Metro, it definitely stands on its own. Its clientele is a mix of rocker types and Cub fans. The bar offers a wide variety of beers and a decent if limited selection of bar food. There are also a few pool tables and a vast array of memorabilia. The latter is quite interesting, reflecting the clientele. Haphazardly sharing space on the walls are autographed photos of base-ball players and rock-and-rollers. And I bet you didn't know this, but the members of the band Metallica are big baseball fans. The little note they scribbled to the owner on their photo makes this clear.

THE CLUBHOUSE

3728 N. Clark Street 773-549-2325
Hours: Mon–Thu, 12 P.M.–10 P.M.; Fri–Sat, 12 P.M.–11 P.M.;
Sun, 12 P.M.–6:30 P.M.

Though the name and management changes, this spot has always functioned as some sort of hipster record or book store. This incarnation is primarily a record store, geared toward the punk/industrial crowd. The goth/industrial CD collection, though not very large, is quite good. This is a great place to look for small label stuff. They also have a section of new vinyl. In addition to the music you'll find a whole slew of T-shirts and lots of punky jewelry—especially spiked collars and wristbands.

METRO

3730 N. Clark Street 773-549-0203
Hours: varies depending on show—rarely open before
6 P.M. and never open past 2 A.M.

A Chicago institution, the Metro has been the city's premiere music venue for years. Big enough to host major national and international acts, the space is also intimate enough so that no such thing as a bad seat exists. Acts as varied as Smashing Pumpkins, The Orb, and David Lee Roth have graced Metro's stage, but for the most part the booking pendulum swings solidly to the side of Smashing Pumpkins and their ilk (on a much smaller scale of course—the Pumpkins can only play special shows here these days). Beer prices are ridiculous, but that's why you should always fill up as best you can at Wrigleyville Tap beforehand.

SMART BAR

3730 N. Clark Street 773-549-4140
Hours: Sun–Fri, 9 P.M.–4 A.M.; Sat, 9 P.M.–5 A.M.

Smart Bar is located below Metro, and although Metro's bouncers herd you here after their performances end, Smart Bar is definitely a "progressive" club in its own right. It is, you might say—though I'm sure you're getting sick of hearing this by now—a Chicago institution. The interior has gotten itself a bit of a glossy makeover, but this is still a worthwhile place to wander down into for both dancing and people-watching. I'd advise you to lay off the mind-enhancing drugs for your visit, however. Smart Bar can be a bit of a meat market, and in bouts of heightened consciousness the desperate courting rituals taking place all about you are only apt to fill you with sorrow and pity for the damnable human race. Stick to the alcohol—that way you don't have to feel any shame until morning over your own pathetic attempts to get laid.

THE GINGER MAN TAVERN

3730 N. Clark Street 773-549-2050
Hours: Sun–Fri, 3 P.M.–2 A.M.; Sat, 3 P.M.–3 A.M.

The Ginger Man is one of those bars that features an entirely eclectic crowd. From yuppies to rockers, Cub Fans to artists, you'll find any and all sorts here. A loud, convivial place, this is a decent joint in which to down a few or shoot some pool.

NUTS ON CLARK

3830 N. Clark Street 773-549-6622
Hours: Mon–Sat, 9 A.M.–4 P.M.; closed Sun

You don't see too many stores like this one. It's a veritable nut warehouse—of the edible variety, of course. Here you can buy bags of peanuts, pistachios, walnuts, chocolate-covered peanuts—you name it. They also have plenty of gift items such as candy and peanut baskets and such. A cool place.

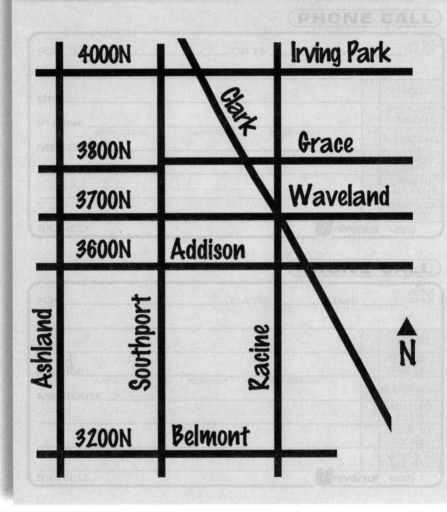

**S
O
U
T
H
P
O
R
T

A
V
E
N
U
E**

Though Southport Avenue has gentrified just like the rest of Lakeview, the speed with which this gentrification took place was astonishing. Back in 1989, I was living on Roscoe just west of Southport. A few blocks west of Clark Street and Wrigley Field, this was a quiet, pleasant, residential neighborhood composed primarily of blue-collar whites along with a small number of Mexican families. Southport Avenue was one of the main commercial strips of the neighborhood, with mom-and-pop type department, hardware, and convenience stores running its length; here and there an upscale establishment had popped up, but these were very much in the minority. There was one particular pizza joint near the "L" station that I used to frequent. During the summer months it was hot and muggy inside, an immense floor fan in the doorway serving as the only air-conditioning. The men in dirty aprons dripping sweat behind the counter were all middle-aged and had the air of taciturn drifters about them. The place was called something like Belli's, and the pizza was bland but edible. It was over the summer when things started changing, with a majority of the old businesses being supplanted by new, yuppified boutiques and cafes. Belli's went out of business with the rest of them. However, a month later it was reopened, still called Belli's. Only now it had been thoroughly remodeled and yuppified. Even so, the same cooks were behind the counter, looking even more dissolute and uncomfortable in their colorful new uniforms. I now became aware of the legend of "Mama Belli." Mama Belli, it turns out, was a much beloved grandmother who had perfected her pizza recipe in the old country using only the finest, freshest ingredients. The Belli family took immense pride in offering her pizza to you, the honored customer, as they had been doing for a number of generations. Or so claimed the slick new take-out menu. Whatever the case, Belli's still turned out the same bland but edible pizza, only now it cost $3 more a pie. My point? Well, I'm not so sure I've actually got one, except to say that Southport Avenue is an extreme case of what can happen to a neighborhood in a very short period of time. Once word gets out about that "hot" new area in which to invest, nothing is safe. But that's life and, I suppose, progress. Southport now boasts a variety of trendy eateries, cafes, and boutiques, catering to the white professionals who have replaced the blue-collar families.

SCHUBAS TAVERN

3159 N. Southport Avenue 773-525-2508
Hours: Sun–Fri, Open for lunch at 11 A.M. (bar opens at 2 P.M.)–2 A.M.; Sat, open till 3 A.M.

Schubas is one of the only spots in the city limits where you can see cutting-edge, country-tinged singer-songwriters and roots music. Separate from the main bar, the music area is quite intimate, sporting a decent-sized stage and good sound system. The kitchen also serves up very good "down home" fare and even offers weekend brunches.

WISTERIA

3715 N. Southport Avenue 773-880-5868
Hours: Thu–Fri, 4 P.M.–9 P.M.; Sat, 12 P.M.–9 P.M.; Sun, 12 P.M.–5 P.M.

Expensive used and vintage women's, men's, and even children's clothes and accessories are the name of the game here. The sort of place you can shop for modern, everyday wear as opposed to many such shops where kitsch is the main selling point.

ARCANUM BOOKS AND CURIOS

3732 N. Southport Avenue 773-528-3433
Hours: Mon–Sat, 11 A.M.–7 P.M.; Sun, 1 P.M.–7 P.M.

 This comfortable little book shop specializes in new age philosophy and healing. Along with incense and various oils, you can also pick up a gift for Baby Jesus as frankincense and myrrh are available.

MUSIC BOX THEATRE

3733 N. Southport Avenue 773-871-6604
Hours: Varies. Check paper or call for show times.

One of the premiere independent cinemas in Chicago, the Music Box features the finest in contemporary, independent releases from all over the world. The main theater harks back to the gilded movie palaces of old and is definitely the most beautiful theater you're likely to see in this age of the cineplex. The Music Box also offers midnight screenings of cult films as well as special showings of old classics.

QUAKE COLLECTIBLES

3759 N. Southport Avenue 773-404-0607
Hours: Closed Mon; Tue–Fri, 1 P.M.–6 P.M.; Sat, 12 P.M.–
6 P.M.; Sun, 12 P.M.–5 P.M.

This small shop carries a wide array of old toys and board games from the '70s and '80s. Haven't played Asteroids since you were a grubby little kid spending your allowance at the local arcade? You can relive those days here—they have a genuine, quarter-guzzling arcade machine in the shop.

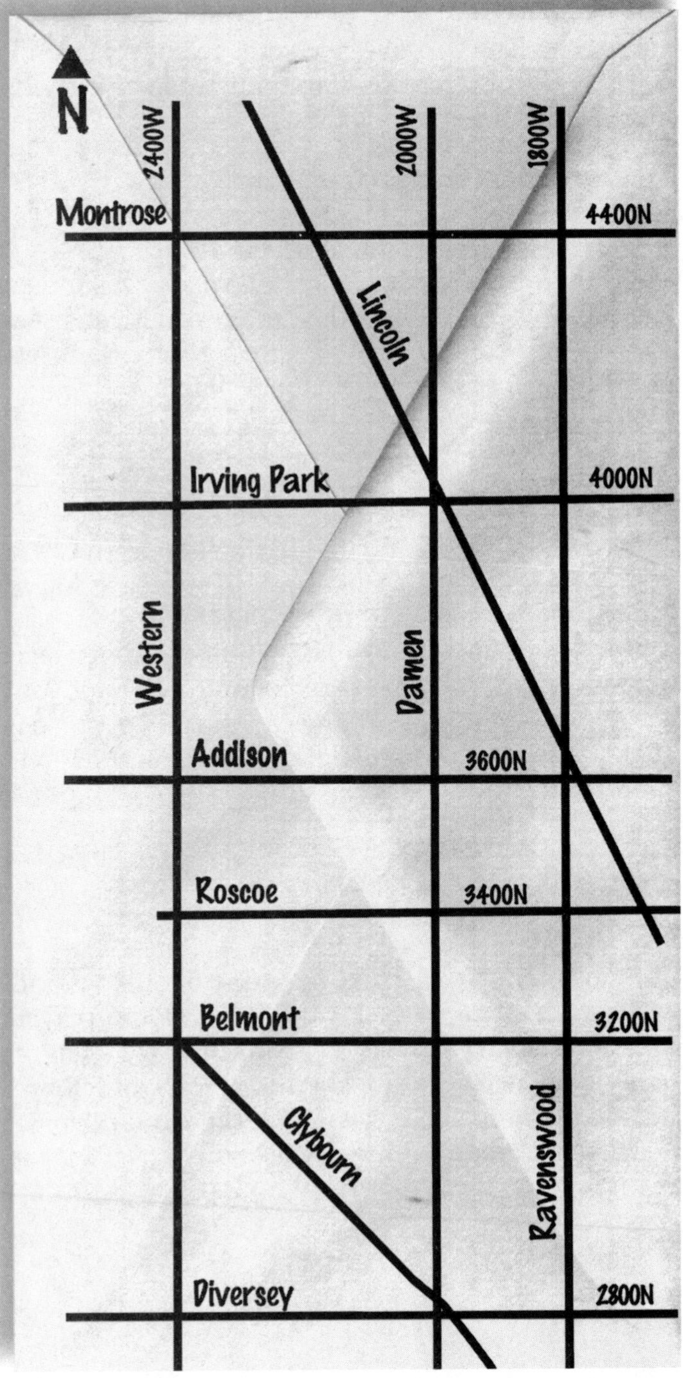
N
2400W
2000W
1800W
Montrose
4400N
Lincoln
Irving Park
4000N
Western
Damen
Addison
3600N
Roscoe
3400N
Belmont
3200N
Clybourn
Ravenswood
Diversey
2800N

N O R T H   C E N T E R

From the early 1900s up to 1968, North Center played host to Riverview, which billed itself as the world's largest amusement park. What will you find in its place now? A strip mall, of course. The amusement park was really the only exciting thing about North Center, which has been primarily residential ever since the first white ethnics began moving out this way in the 1800s. Outside of the commercial strip along Western Avenue, you'll find quiet streets and mixed-income housing. Like the old days, many of the residents are of working-class stock, only now Koreans, Greeks, and Latinos live alongside the whites. There are a few pockets of a more exciting nature in North Center, however. Roscoe Village, St. Ben, and Lincoln Square are three "sub" neighborhoods within the area's boundaries which are described in detail in subsequent chapters. Outside of these particular 'hoods, not a whole lot is going on. Unless, of course, you're into car dealerships and fast food franchises.

GALAXY COMIC ZONE

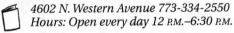

3804 N. Western Avenue 773-267-1043
Hours: Mon–Fri, 12:30 P.M.–7 P.M.; Sat, 11 A.M.–7 P.M.;
Sun, 12:30 P.M.–6:30 P.M.

A nice shop. Here you can get plenty of new comics by the big fellows (Marvel, D.C.) as well as a decent selection of independents. The back issue selection is passable, leaning mainly toward the superheroes.

VARIETY COMICS

4602 N. Western Avenue 773-334-2550
Hours: Open every day 12 P.M.–6:30 P.M.

This small basement shop features the mainstream new titles out there in the comic world, but—unlike many comic shops in the city—they also have a great selection of back issues as well. And what I especially like about the place are all the old issues they carry of my youthful favorite—CONAN! Oh, the hours I'd spend as a flabby, timid, pre-pubescent youth wishing that I, too, could be like this steel-thewed barbarian of the north. But let's not resurrect those grim memories.

oscoe Village, a sub-neighborhood of North Center, perfectly mirrors the changes its neighbor directly to the east, Lakeview, has gone through in population shift. What had once primarily been a neighborhood of blue-collar whites is now filling up with white professionals. This is a pleasant, quiet, residential area. You'll find a small number of shops along the main strip of Roscoe just west of Damen, which share space with a handful of low-key, upscale taverns, cafes, and eateries.

BEAT KITCHEN

2100 W. Belmont Avenue 773-281-4444
Hours: Sun–Fri, 12 P.M.–2 A.M.; Sat, 12 P.M.–3 A.M.

This two-story, upscale neighborhood tavern is a pleasant place to down a few microbrews at the bar or see a local band in the back room. Music is featured nightly. The kitchen churns out high-class bar food, from homemade pizza to burgers and gourmet Italian sausage sandwiches featuring the heftiest shaft of sausage you're ever apt to see.

ROSCOE VILLAGE

SHANGRILA

1952 W. Roscoe Street 773-348-5090
Hours: Mon–Sat, 12 P.M.–7 P.M.; Sun, 12 P.M.–5 P.M.

Small in floor space and selection, Shangrila still manages to boast quite a nice stock. In addition to the usual vintage dresses, coats, and clothing, you can flip through mint-condition magazine ads from the '50s on up. The book section, though relatively small, is alphabetized and full of cheap, quality literature and nonfiction—the best of any vintage shop I've seen.

STERN'S BOOKS

2004 W. Roscoe Street 773-883-5100
Hours: Mon–Fri, 10 A.M.–6 P.M.; Sat, 10 A.M.–4 P.M.; closed Sun

Though I can't say I would entirely agree with the proclamation modestly scripted on the storefront that this is the world's greatest bookstore, I will admit that

Stern's is quite a good one—for psychology. This is their specialty. The shelves are chock full of books on psychological theory, teaching methods, and various disorders. There's also quite a bit of child development material, including games and a few toys.

HARD BOILED RECORDS AND VIDEO

2008 W. Roscoe Street 773-755-2619
Hours: Closed Mon; Tue–Sat, 12 P.M.–10 P.M.;
Sun, 12 P.M.–8 P.M.

This little shop has a bit of everything. Old and new comics, offbeat books and videos, graphic novels, albums, CDs, and cassettes. The Hong Kong video section is their specialty, with plenty of fast-paced, kitschy thrillers in stock. Unfortunately these are only for rental—as are the rest of the videos. Other than the Hong Kong videos you won't find a huge stock of any one particular medium, but there's definitely some quality stuff here.

STELLA DESIGNS

2010 W. Roscoe Street 773-248-9926
Hours: Closed Mon and Tue; Wed–Fri, 12 P.M.–5:30 P.M.;
Sat, 11 A.M.–5 P.M.; Sun, 11 A.M.–4 P.M.

This tiny shop features a smattering of colorful dresses and blouses as well as a large selection of old lunchboxes and a variety of kitschy little items.

VILLAGE DISCOUNT OUTLET

2043 W. Roscoe Street
Hours: Mon–Fri, 9 A.M.–9 P.M.; Sat, 9 A.M.–6 P.M.;
Sun, 11 A.M.–5 P.M.

This one is pleasant and actually somewhat sunny inside, unlike your typical Village Discount. I'm not promising you'll find many treasures here, but you know my policy.

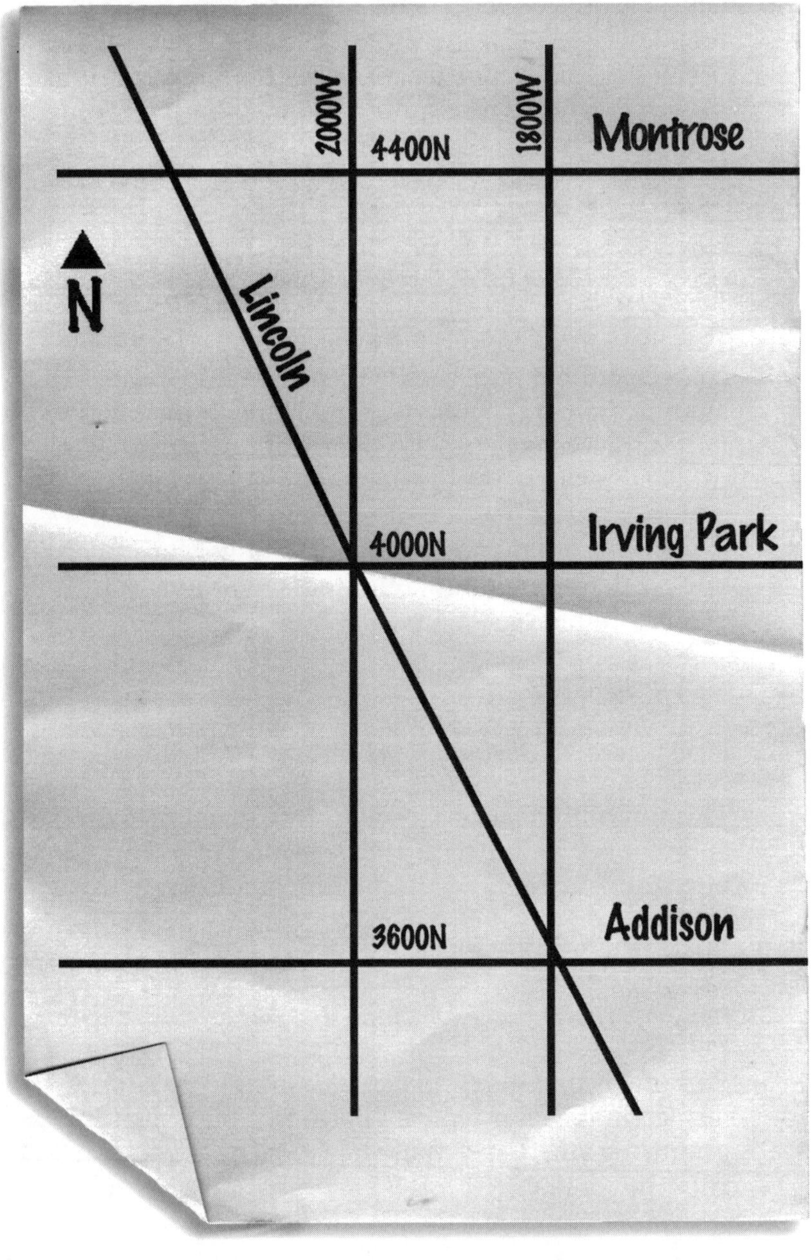
2000W
1800W
4400N
Montrose
N
Lincoln
4000N
Irving Park
3600N
Addison

Named for St. Benedict's Parish and the church built here in 1904, St. Ben's is a quiet, pleasant, North Center neighborhood comprised mostly of white homeowners. Germans were the predominant group here originally, and you'll find a few vestiges of this in a handful of establishments.

MARTYR'S

3855 N. Lincoln Avenue 773-404-9494
Hours: Mon–Tue, 5 P.M.–2 A.M.; closed Wed;
Thu–Fri, 5 P.M.–2 A.M.; Sat, 5 P.M.–3 A.M.; closed Sun

For the longest time I assumed Martyr's was cursed. Back when I first moved into the city many years ago, the building Martyr's occupies was owned by the Moderne Card Co. I telemarketed for this outfit for a few months and did not have a good time. Trying to sell outdated, fifteen-year-old greeting cards sight unseen to florists across the country is not fun. When you did manage to get a sale, the florist would inevitably ship them right back once they got a look at them. A few years back Moderne Card Co. finally met its timely death. In its place sprouted a music venue and restaurant—just like Martyr's. By all accounts this was a decent place with a good crowd. It went out of business almost immediately. So too would Martyr's, I assumed. There was too much bad energy in that place for anyone to ever be able to enjoy themselves in its confines. Surprisingly enough, this has not been the case. You'll find Martyr's a laid-back, decent-enough joint to take in a local band. And Deadheads take notice: a very diligent Dead cover band has taken up a weekly residency here and shows no sign of ever disappearing. These guys are the Civil War reenactors of Dead cover bands, covering specific shows with scary accuracy.

SALVATION ARMY THRIFT STORE

3868 N. Lincoln Avenue 773-528-8893
Hours: Open every day 10 A.M.–5:45 P.M.

You'll find plenty of worthwhile items in this spacious and uncluttered store. Clothes, furniture, records, books—you name it. One of the more pleasant shopping experiences you're likely to encounter in a Salvation Army store.

AUGENBLICK

3907 N. Damen Avenue 773-929-0994
Hours: Sun–Thu, 7 P.M.–2 A.M.; Fri, 3 P.M.–2 A.M.;
Sat, 3 P.M.–3 A.M.

This small, attractive neighborhood bar used to be my hangout several years ago when I lived in the area. Though it is now under different ownership, the old atmosphere is still in place. Here in an intimate, friendly environment, you can take in offbeat bands from the small stage or simply kick back at a table shooting the shit with your buddies. Scores of beers are available, and the hard liquor selection is quite praise-worthy as well.

UNIQUE THRIFT STORE

4112 N. Lincoln Avenue 773-281-1590
Hours: Mon, 9 A.M.–6:45 P.M.; Tue–Sat, 9 A.M.–7:15 P.M.;
Sun, 10 A.M.–5:45 P.M.

Like the Salvation Army store, this is a first-generation resale shop as opposed to a second-generation "vintage" shop. Here in this large, crowded, teeming space, you'll find that most of the better items have already been snatched and are selling for three times as much at a local vintage shop. A lengthy browse is always recommended, however.

GREAT BEER PALACE

4128 N. Lincoln Avenue 773-525-4906
Hours: Mon–Fri, 11 A.M.–2 A.M.; Sat, 11 A.M.–3 A.M.;
Sun, 12 P.M.–2 A.M.

This is the premiere bar in Chicago in which to try imported German beers on tap. The $4 pints might seem expensive, but where else can you drink the likes of Späten Dobblebock and Gösser Dark fresh from the keg? New selections arrive periodically, with seasonal brews always available. Food is served anytime. This is typically bar food, but they do offer items such as German pizza made with bratwurst and nightly dinner specials. You also get free basket of pretzels with mustard. A raucous, fun place. You'll also quickly note that one of the bartenders—Phil—may indeed be Chicago's most opinionated man.

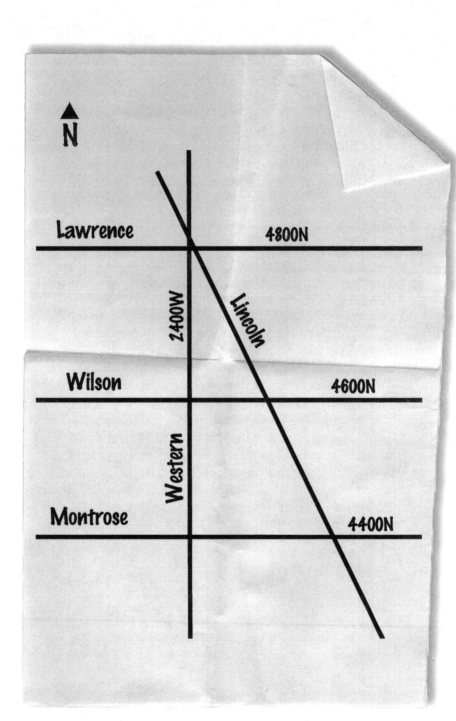

Over the course of the '20s, with the extension of the Ravenswood "L" tracks, lands around Lincoln Avenue, once an old Indian path, began to be heavily settled by families moving away from the congestion of the inner city. Many of them were German, and today they remain the most visible presence in the Lincoln Square area thanks to a small strip of Lincoln at Lawrence that is closed to two-way traffic. Along this strip and farther south of it are a number of German delis, bakeries, restaurants, and gift shops. Greeks settled in this area as well, especially after the building of both the Eisenhower Expressway and the UIC Circle campus in the '60s chopped away all but a small strip of Greektown. Here, along with the essentially German one-way strip of Lincoln, are also a couple of Greek restaurants—with more further south. Plenty of Koreans and Mexicans live in this area now too, but Lincoln Square still manages to be associated primarily with the German shops clustered near the intersection of Lincoln and Lawrence.

LINCOLN SQUARE

GRECIANA TAVERNA

 4535 N. Lincoln Avenue 773-728-1600
Hours: Open every day 11 A.M.–11 P.M.

This Greek restaurant features a cozy, attractive dining room featuring not one but two fireplaces. They also have patio seating during the warmer months. That said, I'll warn you that the regular menu is rather expensive. They do, however, offer a lunch menu. Though limited to only about ten items like souvlaki plates and gyros and such, the prices are very reasonable. And the food is damn good.

OLD TOWN SCHOOL OF FOLK MUSIC

4544 N. Lincoln Avenue 773-728-6000
Hours: Store: Mon–Thu, 10 A.M.–9 P.M.; Fri–Sun, 10 A.M.–
5 P.M. For performances, call ahead or check paper.

A recently transplanted Chicago institution, the Old Town School of Folk Music not only offers classes and hosts performances by national acts, but it also includes a small music shop where you can purchase not just your typical CDs, sheet music, and strings, but banjos as well. Unfortunately, jugs of corn whisky are not available.

DAILY BAR & GRILL

 4560 N. Lincoln Avenue 773-561-6198
Hours: Mon, 4:30 P.M.–11 P.M.; Tue–Thu, 11:30–
11 P.M.; Fri, 10:30 A.M.–12 A.M.; Sat, 10 A.M.–12 A.M.;
Sun, 10 A.M.–10 P.M.

"Nouveau" diners have been big in Chicago for some years with their over-priced "comfort foods" such as meatloaf and pot roast and such. The Daily Bar & Grill does fit into this niche, but their prices are cheaper than most and the grub is very well done. Or at least better than my mom ever made it.

GATE OF DAMASCUS CAFE

 4603 N. Lincoln Avenue 773-907-9677
Hours: Open every day 11 A.M.–10 P.M.

Nothing fancy, this dine-in/carry-out joint serves up very cheap Middle-Eastern fare, mostly in the form of shishkabob sandwiches and such. And as if prices weren't already low enough, they also offer lunch specials. Oh yeah, you can get bagels here too. A Nobel Peace Prize awaits the person who can transfer this idea to Israel.

LAURIE'S PLANET OF SOUND

 4703 N. Lincoln Avenue 773-271-3569
Hours: Mon–Sat, 10 A.M.–10 P.M.; Sun, 11 A.M.–7 P.M.

Though small, this record shop features a little bit of everything. You can find new, used, and import CDs, albums, and cassettes and plenty of quirky videos. This along with sunglasses, T-shirts, a number of books and magazines, and even a few 8-track frickin' tapes! A nice little place.

MEYER DELICATESSEN

 4750 N. Lincoln Avenue 773-561-3377
Hours: Mon–Sat, 9 A.M.–9 P.M.; Sun, 10 A.M.–5 P.M.

This quaint German deli offers a whole lot of stuff. Imported beers, wines, mustards, and chocolates as well as fresh cheese and meats. The quality is impeccable, and you'll be surprised at the variety of bratwurst and liverwurst to choose from. This truly is the land where the braunshwieger grows.

ST. VINCENT DE PAUL THRIFT STORE

4738 N. Western Avenue
Hours: closed Sun; Mon–Sat, 10 a.m.–7 p.m.

This thrift store is large, uncluttered, and very well-organized. You'll find plenty of basic clothing and suits. If you need a plain, white, button-down shirt, well, this place is heaven. All of the sections—men's, women's, and children's—are full of such basic, unexciting items. There's also a large collection of books. But in keeping with the general atmosphere of the store, they're comprised of basic, unexciting titles. Unfortunately that doesn't work as well with books.

Not a whole lot needs to be said about Ravenswood. Though much more residential than St. Ben, it retains the same basic characteristics. Well-kept apartment buildings and houses line quiet, tree-lined streets. At least, they used to be tree-lined. Ravenswood was recently hit by an infestation of the Asian Long-Horned Beetle and hundreds of trees were cut down. This gives Ravenswood's streets an odd look that should continue for some time—older trees interspersed here and there with newly planted saplings. But hey, a hundred years ago Chicagoans would have no doubt welcomed an infestation of beetles compared to an outbreak of yellow fever, so things really aren't that bad when you think about it.

ELITE SPORTSCARD AND COMICS

2028 W. Montrose Avenue 773-784-1396
Hours: Mon–Fri, 11 A.M.–5 P.M.; Sat, 11 A.M.–4 P.M.;
closed Sun

As the store name suggests, this is the place to go if you're into collecting sports cards. They have quite a collection. Other than the cards, you'll find only a small selection of sci-fi memorabilia and toys, as well as current issues of small-press comics.

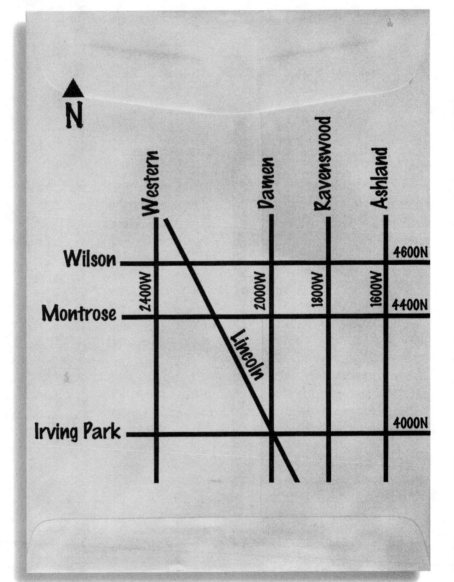

CHRIS AND HEATHER'S RECORD ROUNDUP AND COLLECTIBLES

2034 W. Montrose Avenue 773-271-5330
Hours: Closed Mon; Tue–Sat, 12 P.M.–7 P.M.;
Sun, 12 P.M.–6 P.M.

Legendary Chicago cartoonist and filmmaker Heather McAdams and her husband Chris Ligon own this amusing, fun little shop. The emphasis is definitely on old vinyl, but you can also find a few books, some clothes, and plenty of little toys and knickknacks from days of yore. As far as albums and 45s are concerned, you can find anything from '70s rock to '50s lounge music to Confederate camp songs. No such luck though in finding that rocking ballad of the '60s (1860s, that is) "U. S. Grant Is the Man!"

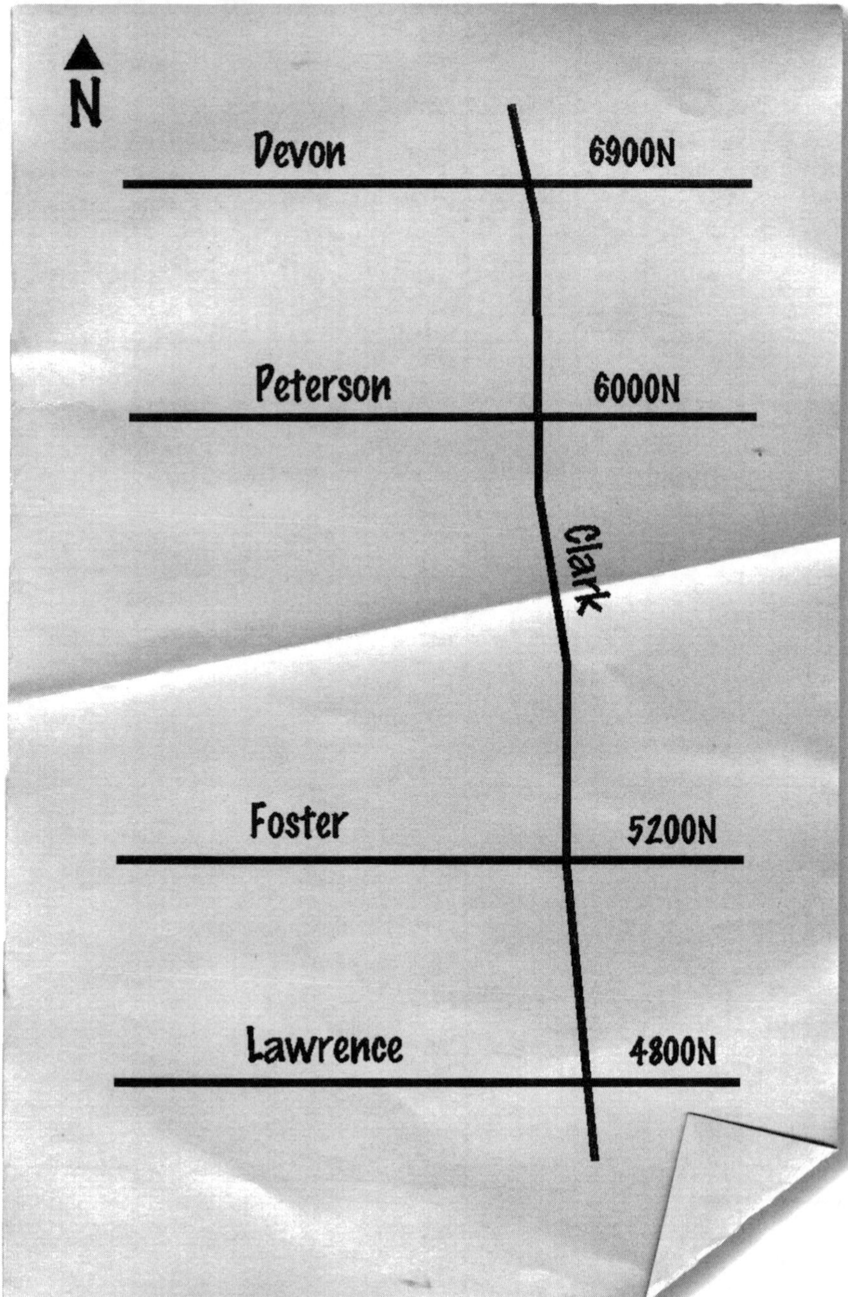

N
Devon
6900N
Peterson
6000N
Clark
Foster
5200N
Lawrence
4800N

In the late 1860s, the area around Clark and Foster was farmland far removed from the city. In the early 1870s, however, many Swedish families, having done well for themselves in carpentry and various other such skilled trades, moved away from the congestion of the city to build homes there. With the arrival of public transportation to the area in 1908, many more Swedes moved to the region and the neighborhood of Andersonville became firmly established. The exclusively Swedish character of this area only lasted into the '30s; different ethnic groups soon began moving in, culminating in the arrival of many Assyrians in the '70s. Today you'll find Andersonville retains aspects of its Scandinavian heritage primarily in a small number of Swedish bakeries and gift shops—along with the Swedish American Museum. These sit alongside a few Japanese restaurants as well as several Middle Eastern eateries and groceries. These days, though, Andersonville is most closely associated with the gay community. Here you'll find a large gay and lesbian population. But unlike Boys Town to the south, you won't find any outrageous clubs. Most people who live here—both gay and straight—tend more toward the bohemian and

ANDERSONVILLE

"intellectual" than residents of Boys Town. What you'll find instead of gay clubs are gay-owned or gay-friendly neighborhood taverns and trendy little restaurants, as well as a number of small theater companies.

VILLAGE DISCOUNT OUTLET

 4898 N. Clark Street
Hours: Mon–Fri, 9 A.M.–9 P.M.; Sat, 9 A.M.–6 P.M.;
Sun, 11 A.M.–5 P.M.

Like most of its cousins, this particular Village Discount is large, crowded, muggy, etc., etc. As usual, most of the contents have been picked over pretty thoroughly, but you never know what you might find.

REALLY HEAVY ANTIQUES

 5142 N. Clark Street 773-784-7936
Hours: Closed Mon and Tue, Wed–Fri, 4 P.M.–7 P.M.;
Sat–Sun, 12 P.M.–7 P.M.

This shop's title may as well refer to the weight of the wad you'll have to fork over for the merchandise. This place sells high-quality antique and vintage furniture from the '40s through the '70s. This is the real stuff, not simply a smattering of kitschy dinner tables from the '70s. If you're looking for high-end furnishings, you can't do much better than this.

OLIVE TREE CAFE

 5200 N. Clark Street 773-561-8105
Hours: Open every day 11 A.M.–10 P.M.

This attractive, colorful, bright, and airy little restaurant serves up decent, reasonably priced Middle-Eastern cuisine. There are plenty of entrées to satisfy both the carnivore and vegetarian.

ANN SATHER RESTAURANT

 5207 N. Clark Street 773-271-6677
Hours: Mon–Fri, 7 A.M.–3:30 P.M.; Sat–Sun, 7 A.M.–5 P.M.

This is Chicago's premiere Swedish restaurant. Sandwich and salad prices are quite reasonable, and though the entrées are a tad more expensive you'll find them worth every penny. The Swedish combo will stuff you to the gills with the likes of Swedish meatballs and potatoes. If this was the fare of the Vikings, I'm jealous. They had all this and ale and debauchery! What a living. Of course the chances were probably pretty good that your skull would get cleaved in two by a battle axe before you were able to collect Social Security, but hell, at least you never had to worry about wearing Depends some day.

SIMON'S TAVERN

 5210 N. Clark Street 773-878-0894
Hours: Open every day 11 A.M.–2 A.M.

This unadorned, simple tavern has recently been sold by the son of the Swedish immigrant who originally owned it, but I'm sure they'll still serve up batches of their famous glogg every Yule season. Believe me, you're not going to find glogg in too many places. And though I'm by no means a glogg expert, I don't imagine you'll find any better than Simon's this side of Minnesota. Definitely a place to stop even in the midst of summer.

THE RIGHT PLACE

 5219 N. Clark Street 773-561-7757
Hours: Mon–Thu, 10 A.M.–4 P.M.; Fri–Sat, 11 A.M.–5 P.M.;
Sun, 12 P.M.–4:30 P.M.

Nothing special, this small resale shop offers the usual fare—men and women's clothing, knickknacks, a smattering of furniture, and books and albums. It's worth a quick browse.

SPECIALTY VIDEO

 5225 N. Clark Street 773-878-3434
Hours: Mon–Thu, 10 A.M.–10 P.M.; Fri–Sat, 10 A.M.–11 P.M.;
Sun, 10 A.M.–10 P.M.

The foreign film section is the pride and joy of Specialty Video, but unfortunately these films are pretty much for rental only. However, they do carry quite a number of independent, offbeat films for sale—both new and used. This is in addition to quality, mainstream films as well. Think of it as your one-stop video shopping joint.

WOMEN AND CHILDREN FIRST BOOKSTORE

5233 N. Clark Street 773-769-9299
Hours: Mon–Fri, 10 A.M.–9 P.M.; Sat, 10 A.M.–7 P.M.;
Sun, 10 A.M.–6 P.M.

This is Chicago's only book shop specializing in women's studies. Within its confines you'll find extensive sections on feminism, gender politics, and lesbian issues. And the children's section just happens to be one of the best in the city. The store also sponsors readings and talks by various authors and professors.

REZA'S RESTAURANT

5255 N. Clark Street 773-561-1898
Hours: Open every day 11 A.M.–12 A.M.

This place is always packed and convivial—at both lunch and dinner time. After eating here you'll know why. Serving up a plethora of Middle-Eastern food— from lamb and seafood to vegetarian dishes and shishkabob platters, Reza's gives you mountains of food for very reasonable prices. You also get a live piano serenade every night. It doesn't get much more civilized than that, now, does it?

CHICAGO RECYCLE SHOP

5308 N. Clark Street 773-878-8525
Hours: Open every day 9 A.M.–6 P.M.

This huge store has an outstanding selection of affordable, quality old furniture, antiques, and jewelry along with typical resale fare such as books and clothing. As for the latter, plenty of fine apparel can be scouted out among the racks.

KOPI: A TRAVELER'S CAFE

5317 N. Clark Street 773-989-5674
Hours: Mon–Fri, 8 A.M.–11 P.M.; Sat, 9 P.M.–12 A.M.;
Sun, 10 A.M.–11 P.M.

This cozy little coffee house bills itself as a traveler's cafe, offering plenty of books and resources on just that topic along with the joe and food. A good place to go and compare notes with fellow travelers. Unfortunately, none of the patrons ever seem all that interested in my war stories even though my latest extensive travels took me as far north as Milwaukee.

MUSICIAN'S NETWORK

5505 N. Clark Street 773-728-2929
Hours: Mon–Fri, 11 A.M.–7:30 P.M.; Sat, 10:30 A.M.–6 P.M.;
Sun, 12 P.M.–5 P.M.

This friendly, laid-back shop is a long-time favorite with many local musicians. Not only do they sell new and used instruments and equipment, but they do fast, quality repair work at fair prices.

SALVATION ARMY THRIFT STORE

5556 N. Clark Street 773-728-8079
Hours: Open every day 10 A.M.–5:45 P.M.

Not the most scintillating jewel in the Salvation Army firmament. You'll find this location crowded, hot, and musty—with most of the contents picked over by vintage-store owners and the hipster neighborhood clientele. But—as usual—it's still worth a look.

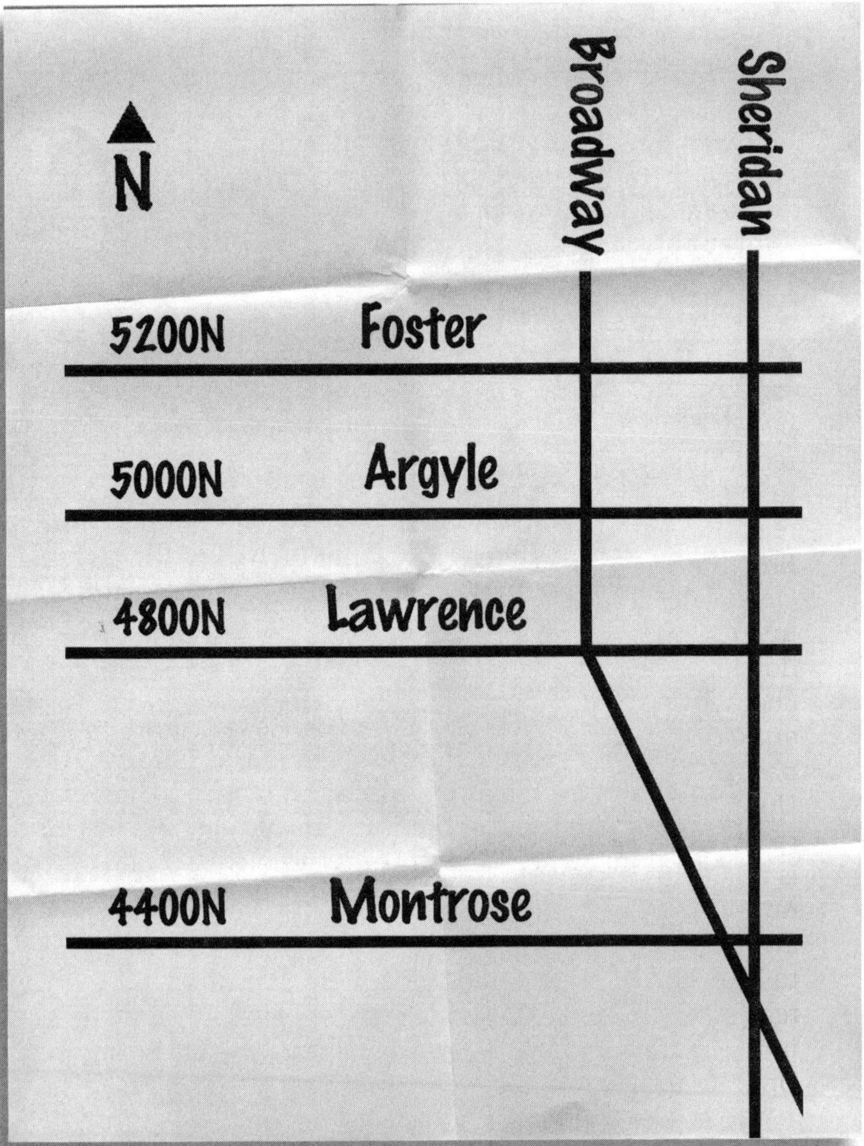
N
Broadway
Sheridan
5200N
Foster
5000N
Argyle
4800N
Lawrence
4400N
Montrose

Uptown is an odd place. I moved to its outskirts back in the mid-eighties at the tender age of nineteen. My apartment was in an area that had more in common with Ravenswood than Uptown really, but the heart of Uptown—Lawrence and Broadway—was only a handful of blocks away. One day I had neither work nor school to occupy my time. Hey, I thought merrily, why not wander down to Lawrence and Broadway—you know, check out the shops and all. Full of enthusiasm and good cheer, I set out. Before an hour had passed I was thoroughly bummed. You see, Uptown had—and still has, though it's been reduced—a large homeless population. The word is that back in the '70s mental institutions could no longer simply lock up their charges and throw away the key. They had to prepare their patients to live in and cope with the real world and then release them. Well, whether they were ready or not, a whole batch of them got released in Uptown.

But that's not all of Uptown's problems. Things started going sour even before World War II. By the '60s Uptown was the destination of all those immigrants and new arrivals who could only afford the cheapest of housing. Things got worse as the government tried to break up the Native American reservation system in an attempt to cure the inhabitants of "Indianness." To do so relocation programs were cooked up—jobs were promised to Native Americans in a variety of cities. Those who took advantage of the program were given a one-way ticket and $50 to reach their destination. And then guess what? There was no job waiting for them after all. Uptown still has a large concentration of Native-Americans, as well as "po' white southern trash," Vietnamese, Filipinos and other southeast Asians, blacks, and Latinos.

Though parts of Uptown have been gentrified (Sheridan Park is what the Realtors call one of these pockets), much of it is still a bit rough around the edges. One interesting development in the area is the establishment of New Chinatown on Argyle just east of Broadway. After the fall of Saigon, many ethnic Chinese living in Vietnam came to Chicago, and here on Argyle you'll find two whole blocks of shops and restaurants, with an emphasis on Vietnamese food and products.

Basically, Uptown is one of those areas that is definitely worth visiting. But, of course, you have to keep your smarts about you. During the day about the worst you'll have to deal with is an occasional panhandler and the smell of urine wafting out of an alley. Things can get a bit more dicey at night since all the bums have gotten even drunker, but plenty of people—suburbanites, natch—mingle about unmolested as a few concert halls are in the neighborhood. So don't be afraid, just be aware. And now I'll stop trying to sound like your parents.

AMERICAN INDIAN GIFT STORE

1756 W. Wilson Avenue 773-769-1170
Hours: Closed Sun and Mon; Tue, 12 P.M.–6 P.M.; closed
Wed; Thu–Fri, 12 P.M.–6 P.M.; Sat, 10 A.M.–6 P.M.

You won't find another store like this in Chicago. This Native American owned and operated shop specializes in pottery, sand paintings, books, cassettes, Kachina dolls, and a variety of other such Native American made and themed items. You'll find everything from cheap souvenir items to expensive, contemporary pieces of art. A very unique Chicago shop.

UNIQUE THRIFT STORE

 4445 N. Sheridan Road 773-275-8623
Hours: Mon–Fri, 9 A.M.–7 P.M.; Sat–Sun, 10 A.M.–5 P.M.

Large, crowded, hot, and picked over, but would you have it any other way? This one happens to have a good-sized parking lot out front so it's much more convenient than others.

TOPPER'S RECORDTOWN

 4619 N. Broadway Avenue 773-878-2032
Hours: Mon–Wed, 10 A.M.–7 P.M.; Thu–Sun, 10 A.M.–6 P.M.

This small, new-and-used music shop specializes primarily in Top 40 soul and R&B. CDs and cassettes only. One cool thing is that most used CDs are only $5.

A-2 WALLIS MILITARY SURPLUS

 4647 N. Broadway Avenue 773-784-9140
Hours: Mon–Thu, 9:30 A.M.–5:45 P.M.; Fri, 9:30 A.M.–
 6:45 P.M.; Sat–Sun, 10 A.M.–5 P.M.

This small surplus shop sells a decent collection of stuff. Pea coats and Air Force sweaters make up the best of the military items, and a great selection of regular boots, jeans, and sweatshirts rounds out the rest of the merchandise. Prices aren't cheap but are reasonable.

AFRICAN WONDERLAND IMPORTS

 4713 N. Broadway Avenue 773-334-2293
Hours: Mon–Fri, 10 A.M.–7 P.M.; Sat, 10 A.M.–5 P.M.;
Sun, 11 A.M.–5 P.M.

This shop features a good selection of African clothing as well as carvings, baskets, and various pieces of folk art. They even sell drums—and at affordable prices.

EQUATOR CLUB

4715 N. Broadway Avenue 773-728-2411
Hours: Wed–Sun, 9 P.M.–2 A.M.

This unique club has been the only one of its kind in Chicago for a number of years. Inside DJs spin Caribbean and Calypso music as well as "Afro pop" and regular old disco. Covers are a bit up there on weekends but not bad at all during the week.

GREEN MILL LOUNGE

4802 N. Broadway Avenue 773-878-5552
Hours: Mon–Fri, 12 P.M.–4 A.M.; Sat, 12 P.M.–5 A.M.;
Sun, 12 P.M.–4 A.M.

 A Chicago legend since 1907, The Green Mill is the sort of dark, smoky, den-like place that is perfect for live jazz. Al Capone used to hang out here, and if it's a slow night you might want to ask if you can see the photo scrapbook behind the bar filled with snapshots of that era. Chicago jazz vocalist Kurt Elling and pianist Willie Pickens play here quite a bit along with many other great musicians. Sunday nights The Green Mill plays host to the famous Uptown Poetry Slam, with live music featured throughout the week. Covers can be a bit steep for particular shows but, what the hell, this place is a national treasure.

SHAKE RATTLE AND READ

4812 N. Broadway Avenue 773-334-5311
Hours: Open every day 12 P.M.–6 P.M.

 This is a fun little shop. Primarily a bookstore, it also carries a hodgepodge collection of albums, cassettes, and CDs. The books are mostly mass-market paperbacks, but there are plenty of worthwhile titles mingled among them. One of the highlights of the shop are the many vintage paperbacks from the '50s sporting lurid covers and suggestive titles such as *Topless Kittens* and *Strange Sisters*. (I'm sure you can guess just how these sisters manifest their "strangeness.")

There are also plenty of current magazines as well as very old back issues, from *Playboy* to *Variety*.

MOODY'S PUB

 5910 N. Broadway Avenue 773-275-2696
Hours: Open every day 11 A.M.–2 A.M.

 If it's a burger you're wanting, this is one of the best places to get it. The burger is Moody's specialty and they do it up right. Hell, even if you don't want a burger but simply want to drink a beer in one of the city's prettiest damn beer gardens, this is the place for you. Watch out for the squirrels, though—they're quite bold. The kitchen's open from 11:30 A.M. to 1 A.M. every day.

NEW CHINATOWN

NHU HOA CAFE

1020 W. Argyle Street 773-878-0618
Hours: Open every day 10 A.M.–10 P.M.

Sporting two elaborate lion statues outside its doors, this pleasant little restaurant serves up Vietnamese and Laotian cuisine. I've only eaten here once and a friend did all the ordering, but everything we sampled—from vegetable dishes to a particularly tasty chicken entrée—was very pleasing to the gullet. The prices are fairly cheap too.

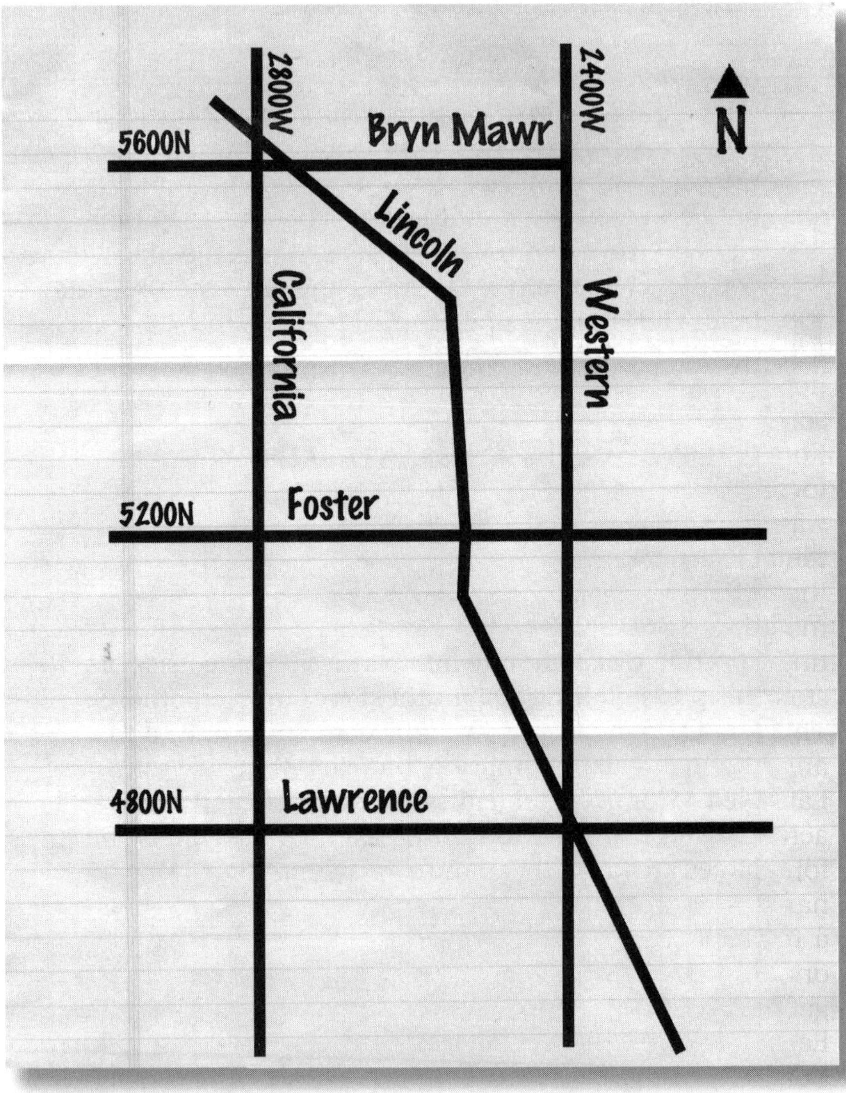
2800W
2400W
N
Bryn Mawr
5600N
Lincoln
California
Western
Foster
5200N
Lawrence
4800N

Korea Town is spread out through the neighborhood of Albany Park, but as there isn't much reason to enter Albany Park except to partake of the Korean culture, Korea Town is all we're going to focus on. A heavily Jewish neighborhood when it was first settled in the early 1900s, Albany Park remained that way up until after World War II. By the early '70s most of the Jewish families had moved to the suburbs and urban decay was setting in. Then the Koreans arrived. Soon scores of storefronts were emblazoned with Korean logos. This pissed off many of the homeowners in the area, who were a smattering of Greek, Polish, and Latino and heavily outnumbered the Koreans actually living in the vicinity. Harmony has been found these days, however, and the neighborhood has shed its somewhat tattered image to become a respectable area, though I must say traffic on one of the main drags—Lawrence Avenue—can get atrocious. Amid many a Greek and Middle-Eastern establishment you'll find dozens of Korean restaurants, groceries, and shops. From stores selling trinkets to auto repair garages, the variety is impressive if not exactly glamorous.

KOREA RESTAURANT

 2659 W. Lawrence Avenue 773-878-2095
Hours: Open 24 hours

This imaginatively titled restaurant is exactly what it purports to be: a Korean restaurant. It's nothing fancy and a bit too brightly lit if you wander in here during the wee hours after a long bender, but the prices are reasonable and you get plenty of appetizers and decent-sized portions. The kalbee is particularly good.

VILLAGE DISCOUNT OUTLET

 3301 Lawrence Avenue
Hours: Mon–Fri, 9 A.M.–9 P.M.; Sat, 9 A.M.–6 P.M.;
Sun, 11 A.M.–5 P.M.

I'm sure you know the score by now. This one is large and cluttered, but no less crowded or slightly moldy smelling. You'll have a somewhat better chance of finding cool knickknacks at this one, but I guarantee nothing.

GARDEN BUFFET

5347 Lincoln Avenue 773-728-1249
Hours: Open every day 11 A.M.–11 P.M.

This spacious restaurant features a huge, tasty-ass buffet, with a wide variety of vegetable and meat dishes, sushi, and raw meats for personal barbecuing. The only problem is that it's very expensive—especially if you do indeed want to make use of the little barbecue pit at the table. Dinners can set you back $17 a person. However, if you go in there at lunch time and don't use the barbecue, you're only looking at about $7 a person. This is well worth it as you'll have no need to eat for the next two days. Get yourself a big ol' bottle of Obee beer as well.

ADAM'S APPLE

 6229 N. California Avenue 773-338-4567
Hours: Open every day 1 P.M.–7 P.M.

This small, ancient head shop has been around since the '60s. Outside of the good collection of bowls and bongs, you can find plenty of T-shirts with nutty slogans and those overly baggy jeans the kids are still in love with these days.

N

2800W

2400W

Devon Avenue   6400N

California

Western

Just west of Western Avenue, Devon becomes one of the city's most interesting streets. Within the span of only a few blocks you'll find a polyglot of cultures. Jewish bookstores and delis; Indian restaurants, electronic stores, and sari shops; Russian bookstores; Pakistani eateries; the Croatian Cultural Center—all call this strip home. You can literally walk for a number of blocks and not hear a word of English. From what I understand Indians from all over the Midwest make shopping pilgrimages here, and many recent immigrants from the various nationalities flock here both to live and shop. If nothing else, you should at least take a drive through.

GANDHI INDIA RESTAURANT

2601 W. Devon Avenue 773-761-8714
Hours: Sun–Fri, 11:30 A.M.–2:30 P.M./5 P.M.–
10 P.M.; Sat, 11:30 A.M.–11 P.M.

In this attractive, casual restaurant, you can get some damn good curries and Tandoori chicken. Plenty of seafood, lamb, and vegetarian dishes are also available at decent, reasonable prices. The Indian beer is also good.

SALVATION ARMY THRIFT STORE

2151 W. Devon Avenue 773-262-3645
Hours: Mon–Fri, 10 A.M.–7:45 P.M.; Sat, 10 A.M.–5:45 P.M.;
closed Sun

This is a good-sized Salvation Army store, and it even
has a parking lot. The predominant item here is clothing, with rack upon rack of standard shirts, pants,
dresses, and jeans for every member of the family. The
emphasis really is on family, for you won't find anything particularly funky here, just regular old clothes. A
decent amount of furniture and housewares is available also, but these fit the same billing as the clothes.

BUNDOO KHAN RESTAURANT

2544 W. Devon Avenue 773-743-6800
Hours: Mon–Fri, 11 A.M.–11 P.M.; Sat, 11 A.M.–12 A.M.;
Sun, 12 P.M.–10 P.M.

This low-key Pakistani restaurant is quite a deal, serving up lunch buffets for $6.99 and dinner buffets for
only a dollar more. There's plenty to choose from for
both the carnivore and the vegetarian, and though I'm
afraid I'm not too familiar with Pakistani food, I did
particularly relish the chicken dish. Chicken Tikka, I
believe it was called. Or perhaps, simply Tikka chicken.
Whatever the case, it sure was good. This is a great
place to fill up the innards on the cheap.

THE RUSSIAN-AMERICAN BOOKSTORE

2746 W. Devon Avenue 773-761-3233
Hours: Open every day 10 A.M. to 7 P.M.

Here you'll find a large collection of books, magazines,
and newspapers, along with a variety of knickknacks,
dolls, and—to use a phrase those French-speaking
Czarist oppressors of old would've enjoyed—objets
d'art. Unfortunately for those of us who have no com-
prehension of Russian, most of the reading material is
indeed in that language. However, the charming old
proprietor will be more than happy to direct you to the

small collection of English-language books in stock. And not only will he suggest a few selections, he'll tell you a few tales of the old country as well. An interesting little shop.

NEW YORK KOSHER SAUSAGE CORPORATION

2900 W. Devon Avenue 773-338-3354
Hours: Sun, 8 A.M.–6 P.M.; Mon–Wed, 8 A.M.–7 P.M.;
Thu, 8 A.M.–9 P.M.; Fri, 8 A.M.–6 P.M.; closed Sat

Don't let the foreboding, official-sounding name fool you—this is nothing but a small, neighborhood grocery. The meat counter in the back is what sets it apart from other such shops. Here you can get decent, reasonably priced, no-frills sandwiches. Pastrami and corned beef are the specialties of course, but if you've got a hankering for a plain old baloney sandwich, you can indulge that urge here as well.

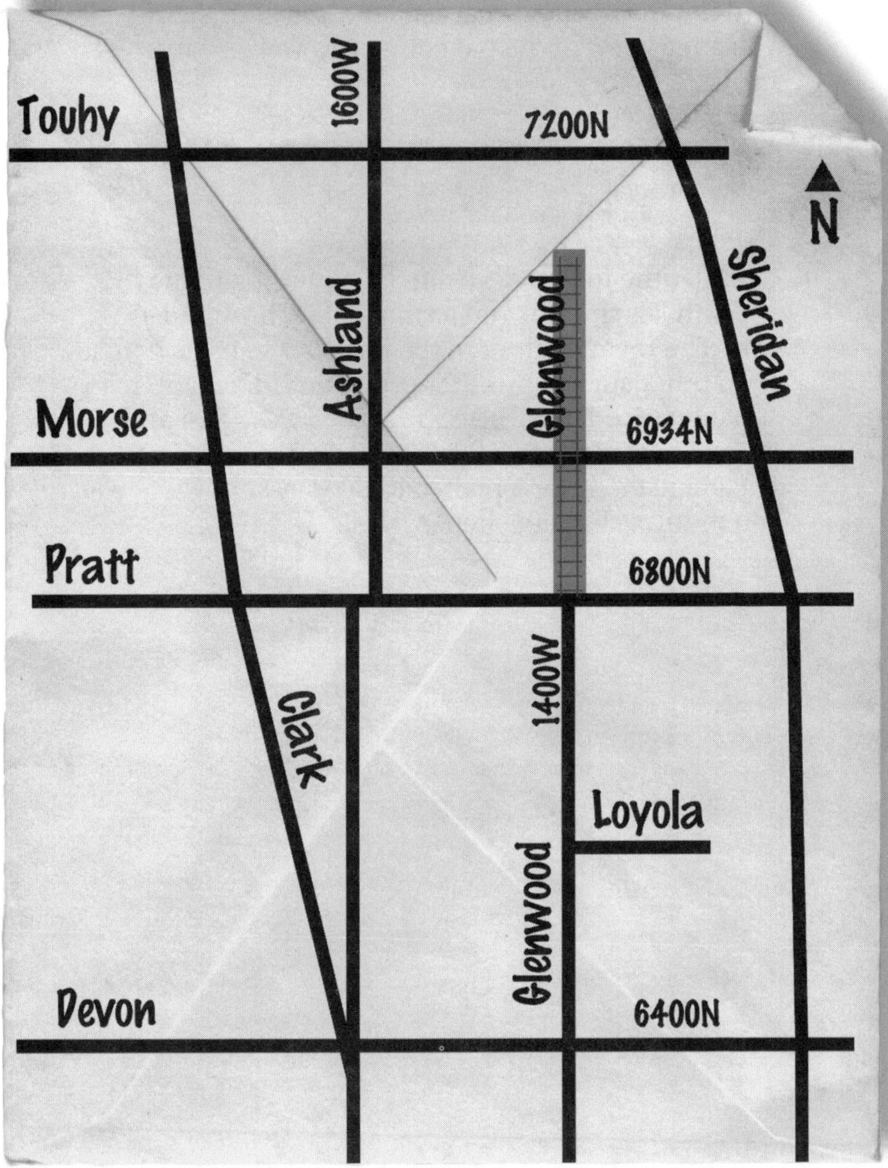
Touhy
1600W
7200N
N
Sheridan
Ashland
Glenwood
Morse
6934N
Pratt
6800N
1400W
Clark
Loyola
Glenwood
Devon
6400N

ROGERS PARK

The last stop before the border of Evanston, Rogers Park is a widely varied neighborhood. Rogers Park, originally home to middle-class Swedes and Irish, was incorporated into Chicago in 1893. An influx of Orthodox Jewish families began arriving in the '20s. By the '60s, the western part of the neighborhood was primarily Jewish, with a very strong presence remaining to this day. To the east things are different—and a little bit shady, though not to the degree they were some ten years ago, when a late-night stroll home from the Morse "L" could occasionally fill the air with a heavy dose of what can only be called "bad vibes." East Rogers Park is very diverse, its population made up of every ethnic and income group you can think of. Near the lake are expensive homes and apartments. Not far away are low-income housing and even projects. I lived in Rogers Park back in 1990, in a building full of other white, college-age residents like me. Next door was a halfway home for the mentally ill. Across the street was a low-income apartment building. The rest of the block was filled with middle-class, mostly white homeowners—a smattering of minority families among them. This is a pretty fair indication of how the neighborhood is comprised, though these days—like most areas of the north side— things are gentrifying, with property values going up and the "lower classes" being shunted aside. You also have plenty of college students roaming around since Loyola University is nearby. A large hippie community used to exist here at one time, and vestiges of that can still be found in the neighborhood. Though a bit out of the way, Rogers Park is definitely one of the more unique areas of the city. And surprisingly enough, its many small, unheralded beaches are among some of the nicest in the city.

THE FACTORY THEATRE

 1257 W. Loyola Avenue 773-274-1345
Hours: Varies. Check paper or call ahead for show times.

This is a small, offbeat company with a heavy emphasis on campy humor. The titles of a few of their most recent productions—*White Trash Wedding* and *The Barbara Walters Interviews*—says it all.

LEONA'S RESTAURANT

 6935 N. Sheridan Road 773-764-5757
Hours: Mon–Thu, 11 A.M.–11 P.M.; Fri–Sat, 11 A.M.–1 A.M.;
Sun, 12 P.M.–11 P.M.

As you're no doubt already aware, this small, family-owned chain of restaurants serves up what I consider to be Chicago's best thin-crust pizza. Dining in is always a casual, pleasant experience. Besides the pizza you can get full dinners—pasta to seafood—as well as an excellent selection of specialty sandwiches.

VIBES MUSIC

 6736 N. Sheridan Road 773-465-9056
Hours: Sun–Thu, 10 A.M.–8 P.M.; Fri–Sat, 10 A.M.–10 P.M.

This mid-sized, sunny shop features a decent new and used CD selection along with a few cassettes.
Emphasis is on rock, but they do stock plenty of jazz, techno, and hip hop.

ATOMIC CAFE

 6746 N. Sheridan Avenue 773-764-9988
Hours: Sun–Thu, 10 A.M.–12 A.M.; Fri–Sat, 10 A.M.–1 A.M.

 This Loyola hangout is an attractive place to knock back a cup of coffee or down a sandwich. Ice cream is also available, along with a small browsing library. You can even hop onto the Internet if one of the two computers is free. The cafe especially comes in handy if you're going to see a flick at the Village North, a second-run theater. You can either get up from one of the outdoor tables and stride a few feet to its entrance, or proceed directly inside from an entrance in the cafe.

THE ARMADILLO'S PILLOW

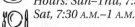 *6753 N. Sheridan Road 773-761-2558*
Hours: Closed Mon; Tue–Fri, 2 P.M.–8 P.M.; Sat, 12 P.M.–
8 P.M.; Sun, 12 P.M.–5 P.M.

This is a small, attractive used bookstore. The decor will make you think you stepped into a beautiful, hippie acid fantasy. No real specialization, but a decent enough general selection of both fiction and nonfiction.

UNAN IMPORTS

6971 N. Sheridan Road 773-274-4022
Hours: Mon–Sat, 11 A.M.–7 P.M.; Sun, sometimes 1 P.M.–
5 P.M., sometimes closed

This shop offers a large collection of African carvings, jewelry, and crafts. The prices are quite reasonable and there are a number of very beautiful pieces here. A unique little place.

ENNUI CAFE

 6981 N. Sheridan Road 773-973-2233
Hours: Sun–Thu, 7:30 A.M.–11 P.M.; Fri–
Sat, 7:30 A.M.–1 A.M.

Bright, airy, and homey, this pleasant cafe allows you plenty of space in which to spread out. Fresh juice, bagels, and assorted pastries and sandwiches are offered along with the java. And let me tell you—they make a mean tiramisu. Outside seating is available during the warmer months.

THE NO EXIT CAFE

 6970 N. Glenwood Avenue 773-743-3355
Hours: Open every day 4 P.M.–12 A.M.

Not only is The No Exit one of the best cafes in the city, but it is a Chicago institution, having been around for years. A funky, cluttered, comfortable little place, its hippie origins are still visible. There are performances practically every night, from music to improv theater and poetry readings. You can also browse through a number of books up front while waiting on a meal. The menu is very extensive for a place of its size. A very friendly, relaxing place.

HEARTLAND CAFE

 7000 N. Glenwood Avenue 773-465-8005
Hours: Mon–Fri, 7 A.M.–2 A.M.; Sat, 8 A.M.–3 A.M.;
 Sun, 8 A.M.–2 A.M.

Though some might disagree on labeling this place a Chicago institution, they definitely can't deny it its status as a Rogers Park institution. A combination cafe/general store/bar/restaurant/club, the Heartland features an extensive, reasonably priced, vegetarian-friendly menu, a good selection of beer, and nightly music. The acts range from jazz to world beat to '70s R&B cover bands. A very friendly place, it's the sort of joint to hit when you're tired of feeling cynical and jaded. And that's why you should never come here with my old buddy Mikey, who tends to personify those traits. The only time I've ever seen anyone get angry at this bastion of good vibes was because of him. While chatting with a nice, older hippie woman, he uttered a snort of contempt when she mentioned with pride that her father had played for the NBC Orchestra. "That's just a TV orchestra," he muttered. Whoo boy, when a hippie gets violent it's never pretty.

TURTLE ISLAND BOOKS

7001 N. Glenwood Avenue 773-465-7212
Hours: Closed Mon; Tue–Sat, 11 A.M.–7 P.M.;
Sun, 12 P.M.–6 P.M.

This attractive, new-and-used bookstore specializes in new-age spirituality. You can also buy incense, oils, and crystals here as well as get a tarot reading. And say hello to the smart-ass parakeet in the corner.

MORSELAND MUSIC ROOM

1218 W. Morse Avenue 773-764-6401
Hours: Sun–Fri, 8 P.M.–2 A.M.; Sat, 8 P.M.–3 A.M.

This is a comfortable place to kick back and catch a local band. Though the space isn't very large, plenty of tables are set up about the stage, so you can usually get a seat when you're in the mood to simply sit and observe. A very unpretentious joint.

RECORD EXCHANGE

1505 W. Morse 773-973-0452
Hours: Mon–Sat, 11 A.M.–8 P.M.; Sun, 12 P.M.–6 P.M.

The front windows of this used record shop are plastered with posters of hip-hop and R&B artists. However, it certainly doesn't specialize in such. Along with a few selections of the above you get mostly rock and jazz. The CD selection is decent, but the vinyl and cassette inventory is enormous.

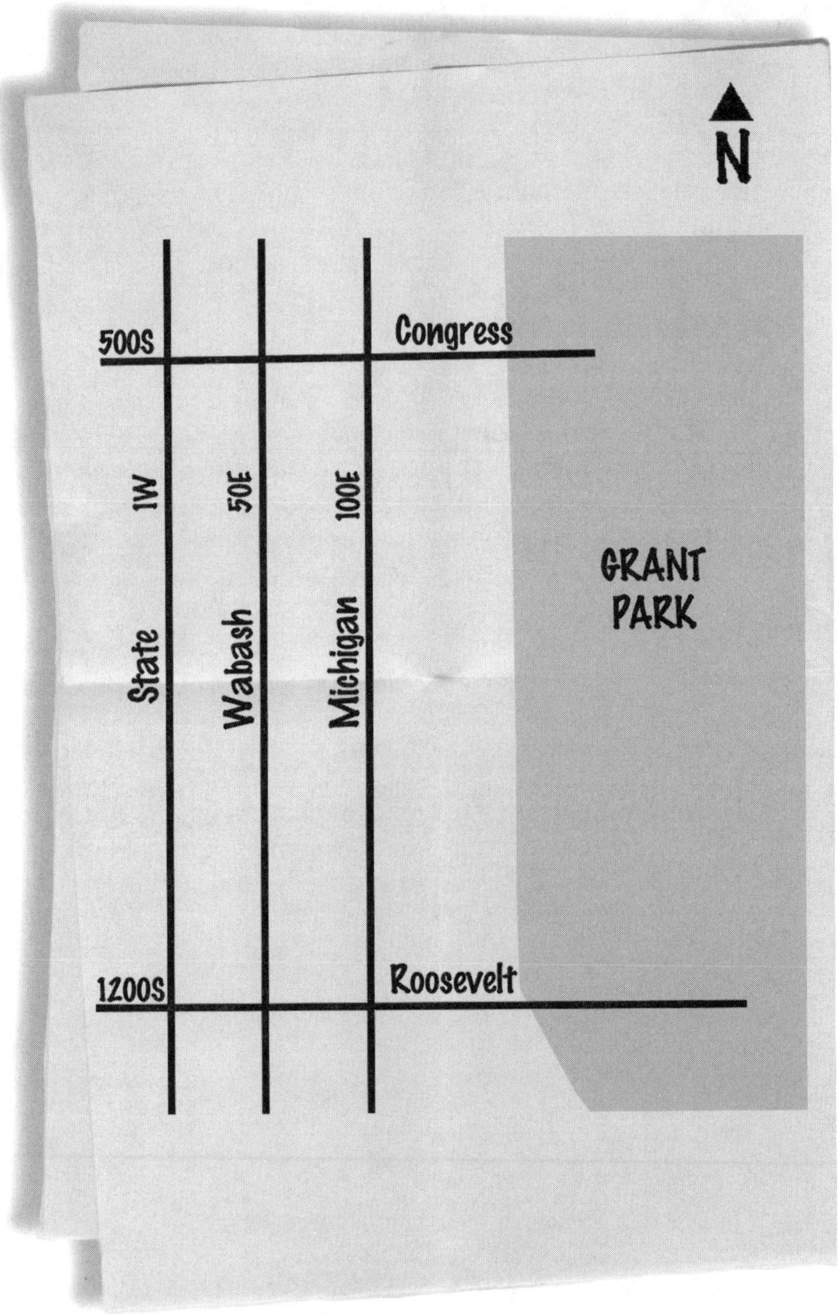
N
Congress
500S
1W
50E
100E
State
Wabash
Michigan
GRANT PARK
Roosevelt
1200S

The South Loop is much more sedate than the Loop proper. Many condos are popping up in place of the S.R.O. (single room occupancy) hotels that used to be peppered liberally through the area. Consequently some night life is beginning to appear, but for the most part you'll find the South Loop relatively quiet, with a number of low-key businesses spread throughout. Roosevelt University and my own alma mater—Columbia College—are in the South Loop, as well as the Sperticus Museum of Judaica, the Shedd Aquarium, the Field Museum, and the Adler Planetarium.

SANDMEYER'S BOOKSTORE

714 S. Dearborn Street 312-922-2104
Hours: Mon–Wed, 11 A.M.–6:30 P.M.; Thu, 11 A.M.–
8 P.M.; Fri, 11 A.M.–6:30 P.M.; Sat, 11 A.M.–5 P.M.;
Sun, 12 P.M.–5 P.M.

This is a sleekly designed, sunny store with a decent general selection of new books. No particular section is all that large, but what they do stock is all quality stuff—no Tom Clancy or Danielle Steele here. They also sell postcards and "artsy" greeting cards.

BUDDY GUY'S LEGENDS

754 S. Wabash Avenue 312-341-0748
Hours: Mon–Thu, 5 P.M.–2 A.M.; Fri, 4 P.M.–2 A.M.;
Sat, 5 P.M.–3 A.M.; Sun, 6 P.M.–2 A.M.

One of Chicago's best blues clubs, this place is indeed part-owned by Chicago legend Buddy Guy. Live music is featured every night, and many of the acts passing through are nationally known. They also serve up cajun food until midnight. This is some good, classic stuff: jambalaya, red beans and rice, and fried catfish. They also serve po' boys, but I must say I'm a bit leery of their authenticity since they're served open-faced.

HOT HOUSE

31 E. Balbo Drive 312-362-9707
Hours: Open every day 6 P.M.–2 A.M.

Located originally in Wicker Park, Hot House went on hiatus for a while before hooking up with these new digs. They seem to have made themselves comfortable here and will hopefully remain for a long time. Hot House is the place to go for world music. African and Latin American musicians play here regularly, and they also host plenty of jazz bands in between. In addition, they stage plays, film screenings, and readings—not to mention various workshops. Think of Hot House as your all-purpose arts complex.

POWELL'S BOOKSTORE

828 S. Wabash 312-341-0748
Hours: Mon–Fri, 10:30 A.M.–6 P.M.; Sat, 10 A.M.–6 P.M.;
Sun, 12 P.M.–5 P.M.

Though larger, this Powell's is not all that different from the others in the city. Upstairs you'll find the big-ticket art books and newer fiction and such. Downstairs, hell, it's a virtual warehouse. Row after row of books spread out around you, along with discount tables. You could literally spend an entire day here and still only scratch the surface.

This is only a tiny remnant of the original Greek Town that began taking form in the late 1890s. The establishment of the Eisenhower Expressway and the UIC campus pared it down to what it is today—essentially just a three-block strip of Halsted from Adams on the north to Jackson on the south. Greek Town used to be an informal sort of place in which to hang out. I remember going there with my sisters for Easter when I was eighteen. I wanted to order wine with my dinner but decided against it since I was, of course, underage. When I ordered a Coke, the waiter frowned distastefully and told me I would have wine instead. I didn't argue with him. In 1996, Chicago hosted the Democratic National Convention at the United Center, and since Greek Town isn't far from there, it was somewhat spruced up along with the preparations for the national event. You'll now find a few Athens-like columns sprouting up on a couple of corners. But they didn't stop there. Some of the restaurants disappeared, and the ones remaining got major facelifts. They've become upscale. Gone are the days when you could feel comfortable stumbling into one of these joints dressed in a T-shirt and pair of shorts and dine

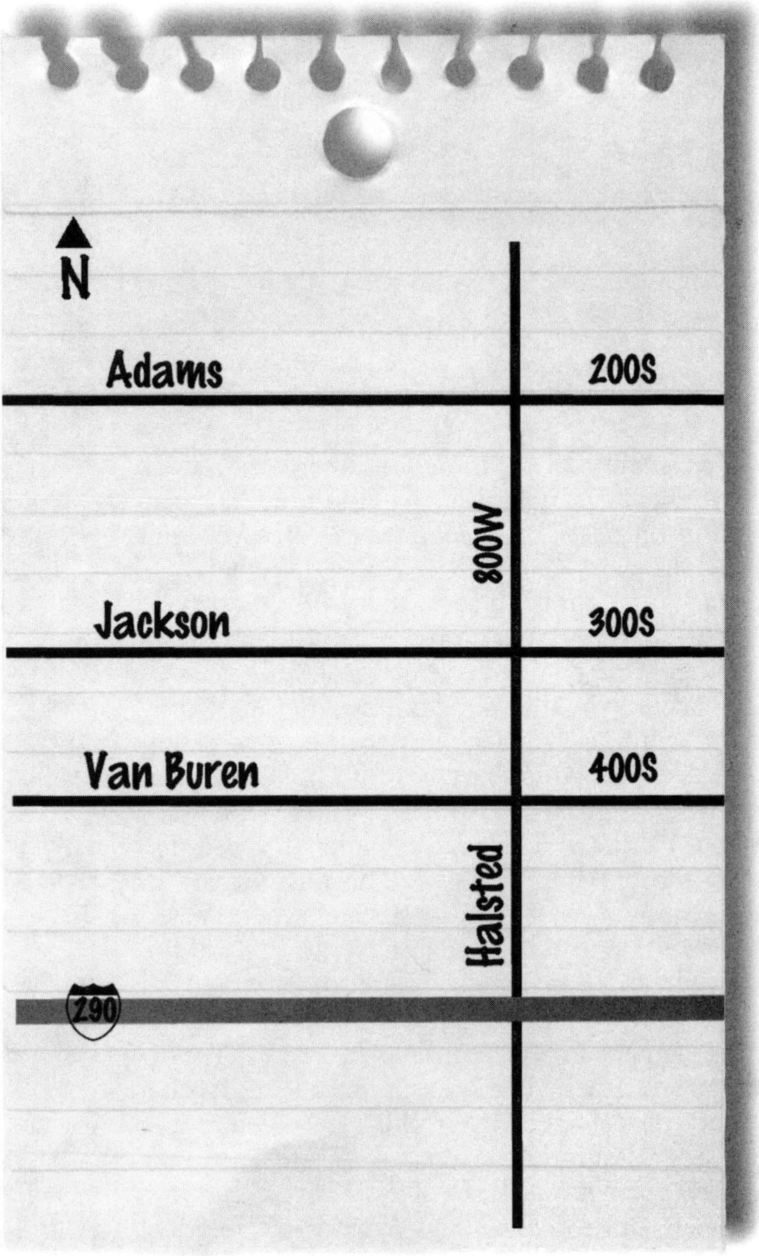

N
Adams
200S
800W
Jackson
300S
Van Buren
400S
Halsted
290

alongside nattily attired businessmen and their wives. Yet the food in these places is still excellent, and you can certainly force yourself to don more presentable clothing in order to have a go at it. But if you're underage and ask for a bottle of wine these days, expect to get carded.

CHRISTIAN INDUSTRIAL LEAGUE RESALE SHOP

112 S. Halsted Street 312-421-2420
Hours: Tue–Sat, 9 A.M.–4:30 P.M.

 This is your basic resale shop. A smattering of very normal clothes and a large selection of dishes and drinking glasses are about all you're gonna get here.

ATHENIAN CANDLE COMPANY

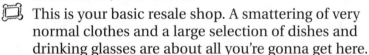
300 S. Halsted Street 312-332-6988
Hours: Mon–Tue, 9:30 A.M.–6 P.M.; closed Wed; Thu–
Fri, 9:30 A.M.–6 P.M.; Sat, 9:30 A.M.–5 P.M.; closed Sun

This candle shop is the real thing—they make them right in the back room. Here you can buy candles for whatever you desire—for wealth, love, or general happiness. This is primarily a religious shop—but not in a Christian or Pagan or Greek Orthodox or New Age or any other sort of easily identifiable way. Along with the multitude of candles are oils and incenses, icons, prayer and blessing cards, and various other spiritual doodads. Prices range from expensive to ridiculously cheap. You can actually buy candles as long as your arm for six bucks. And these aren't crappy ones that immediately sputter and die either. A very interesting place.

ZORBA'S

301 S. Halsted Street 312-454-0784
Hours: Open 24 hours

My favorite place for gyros, Zorba's still retains its somewhat gritty atmosphere. Here you'll find a large selection of food, from the aforementioned gyros to full-on Greek dinners to burgers and hot dogs. Zorba's comes in most handy for carry-out after 2 A.M. when you're looking to sop up the beer with some meat and grease. During more respectable hours when it's not so crowded, however, you can easily get a table or hang out with the old timers at the bar in back.

THE PARTHENON RESTAURANT

314 S. Halsted Street 312-726-2407
Hours: Open every day 11 A.M.–1 A.M.

My favorite Greek Town restaurant, The Parthenon has been remodeled and looks quite swank. As I mentioned earlier, most of these restaurants have classed up their images and atmospheres in the last few years. Dining here is still casual, only now I wear a decent shirt and pair of jeans and try to be reasonably sober. The food is outstanding—especially the lamb dishes. And the potatoes, of course. The Greeks really have a way with potatoes, don't they? In addition you'll find a whole slew of items on the menu, from seafood to steaks to broiled quail. Prices aren't cheap, but they're not so steep that you can't order a bottle of wine with your meal. And the food is definitely worth the dent in your wallet.

Uust like Greek Town, this is only a small remnant of the original Little Italy, though the Italians managed to retain a bit more territory than the Greeks. This area grew from a rough ghetto populated by immigrants from southern Italy into a respectable, middle-class neighborhood full of well-kept houses and yards. So imagine the surprise of the residents when they discovered most of the neighborhood was to be stamped out to make way for the University of Illinois Circle Campus. Mayor Richard J. Daley refused to hear their pleas and sent them packing back in the early '60s.

Little Italy today is indeed populated by Italians—they don't just run the delis, restaurants, and shops along Taylor Street. As this is a very sedate, safe neighborhood, it might come as a surprise to learn that projects sit right smack in the middle of it. Apparently these aren't a source of trouble to the neighborhood at all. Of course this leads to jokes about the mob policing the streets, but I wouldn't put much stock in it. My mother's side of the family is as Italian as they come—my grandparents grew up in the general area—and their closest mob connection is the close proxim-

LITTLE ITALY

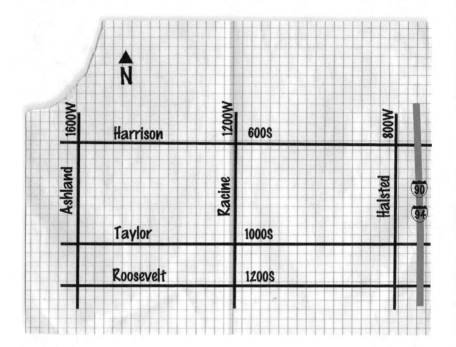

ity of Al Capone's grave to that of my great-grandmother's. Chicago Italians, I might add, are very sensitive about being compared to mobsters. You should have heard the hullabaloo they raised in protest over the touristy Al Capone "museum" that lived a short life in River North back in the mid-'90s.

AL'S #1 ITALIAN BEEF

1079 W. Taylor Street 312-226-4017
Hours: Mon–Sat, 9 A.M.–1 A.M.; closed Sun

A Chicago institution, Al's has been serving up Italian beef for quite some time. Prices have gone up over the years, but for only a few bucks you can still get a heaping, weighty hulk of an Italian beef sandwich that will fill you up good and proper. They also serve your typical burgers and such, but the Italian beef is definitely the must-try.

MARIO'S LEMONADE STAND

 W. Taylor Street in the middle of the block between Aberdeen and Carpenter.
Hours: Open May to October, every day 10 A.M.–10 P.M.

Another Chicago—not just a Taylor Street—institution. Mario's serves up the best Italian Ice you're ever apt to have the pleasure of eating, chock-full of real fruit. You'll always find lines of people, but you can order the stuff by the gallon and keep it in your own freezer if you're so inclined. No summer is complete without at least one pilgrimage to Mario's.

FALBO'S DELI

 1335 W. Taylor Street 312-421-8915
Hours: Mon–Sat, 10 A.M.–3:30 P.M.; closed Sun

This small deli has been around since 1912. Here you can get some tasty sandwiches. And though I know this is an Italian deli, I must say I'm particularly fond of their American sub. You can also buy lunch meats, cheeses, and oils here. There's also a few tables for in-store dining.

LEONA'S RESTAURANT

 1419 W. Taylor Street 312-850-2222
Hours: Mon–Thu, 11 A.M.–11 P.M.; Fri–Sat, 11 A.M.–1 A.M.; Sun, 12 P.M.–11 P.M.

As I've rhapsodized a number of times already, this small, family-owned chain of restaurants serves up what I consider to be Chicago's best thin-crust pizza. Dining in is always a casual, pleasant experience. Besides the pizza you can get full dinners— pasta to seafood—as well as an excellent selection of specialty sandwiches.

GRAND AVENUE

BARI FOODS

1120 W. Grand Avenue 312-666-0730
Hours: Mon–Sat, 8 A.M.–6:30 P.M.; Sun, 8 A.M.–1 P.M.

Right next door to D'Amato's Bakery, Bari's is a family-owned Italian grocery and butcher shop. They also make one of the most addictive, spicy Italian subs I've ever had. They must put lithium in that thing. The prosciutto and fresh mozzarella sandwich is quite good as well. Bari's also sells beer and wine, produce, plenty of imported, canned Italian delicacies, and a whole messload of pasta. The store is too small to sport any tables, but if you're passing through the area, this is one of the best places to pick up a sandwich. But keep in mind, when you order a hot sandwich, you can damn well bet it's going to be hot. And we're not talking temperature-wise either. These subs are so spicy they'll have you sucking air like a nitrous freak.

Maxwell Street is the most well-known thoroughfare in a neighborhood that used to be called Jew Town. Back around the turn of the century, the area was an intensely overcrowded ghetto packed with thousands of Jewish Eastern European immigrants. Jewish shops and eateries dominated the neighborhood, along with hundreds of vendors selling fruits, vegetables, knives, trinkets, and other such merchandise from hand-pulled carts. From this emerged the outdoor Maxwell Street Market. In only a decade, many Jewish families had saved enough money to move, yet most merchants retained their shops in the area. The neighborhood then became host to a large concentration of African-Americans, and it was here that the Chicago blues sound became defined, with bands jamming at the market.

These days the Maxwell Street Market has been removed a mile east to Canal Street. Good ol' UIC wanted the land for parking lots. What you'll find now on this two-block stretch of Halsted between Roosevelt and Maxwell are a slew of clothing stores operated primarily by Arabic merchants. These shops cater to the residents of the projects directly west, selling everything from

MAXWELL STREET

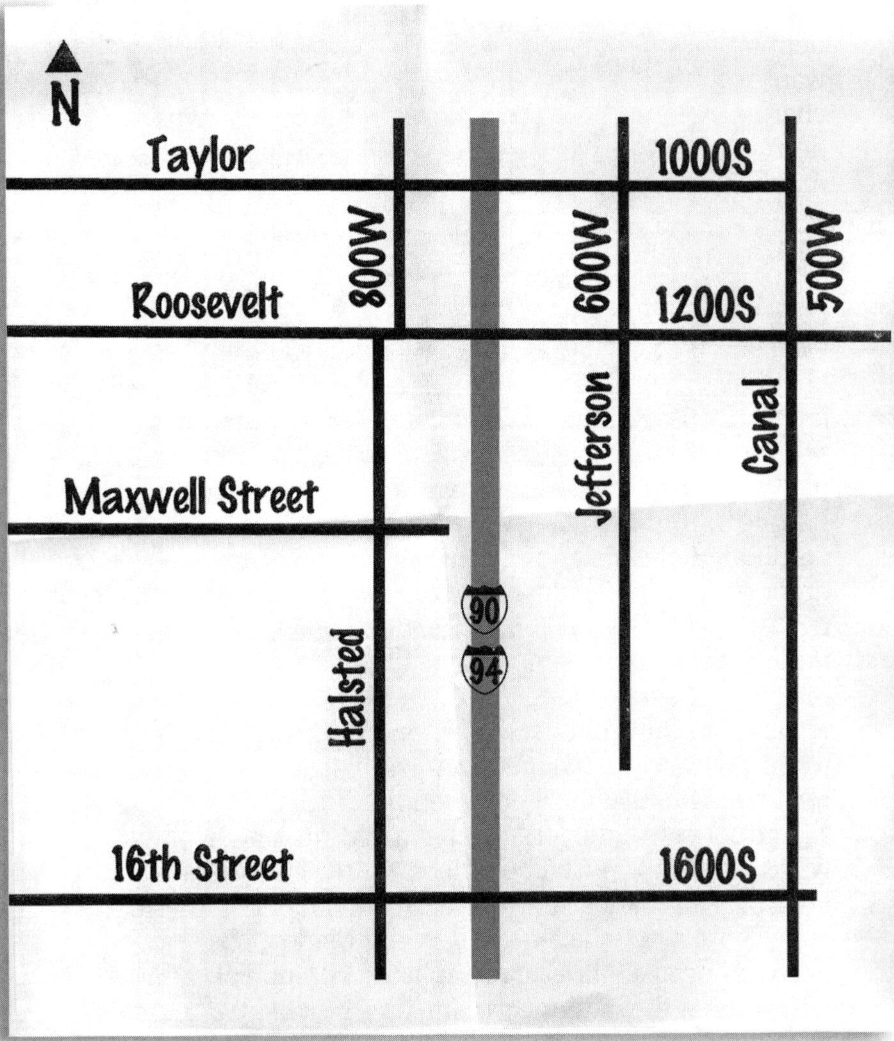

N
Taylor
1000S
800W
600W
500W
Roosevelt
1200S
Jefferson
Canal
Maxwell Street
90
94
Halsted
16th Street
1600S

sportswear to fancy duds. Unfortunately, by the time you read this all these shops may be gone. UIC wasn't satisfied with their parking lots. They want it all now. If all goes the way they desire, the entire area will be razed to the ground to make way for student dorms and private condos. And if UIC got its way when it wanted to displace middle-class Italian and Greek families, the chances are just shy of phenomenal that it'll be allowed to destroy a bustling shopping district catering to poor African-Americans.

MAXWELL STREET MARKET

Canal Street between Taylor Street and 16th Street
Hours: Every Sunday rain or shine from (officially)
7 A.M.–3 P.M.

Though a pale copy of the original Maxwell Street Market a mile to the west, this is still a colorful place to be on Sundays. You still have musicians jamming and plenty of food stalls grilling up goodies. And the range of merchandise is still impressive. Here you can barter for anything from tools and tires to fruits and vegetables, clothing and stereo equipment, and books and mouthwash. The Maxwell Street Market is a living bit of Chicago history—bastardized history at this point, but history all the same.

MANNY'S COFFEE SHOP & DELI

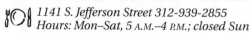 *1141 S. Jefferson Street 312-939-2855*
Hours: Mon–Sat, 5 A.M.–4 P.M.; closed Sun

In business since 1942 and always hopping with customers, Manny's is an old style Jewish cafeteria that's hardly changed since the day it opened. Manny's serves up everything from bacon and eggs to Salisbury steaks and Hungarian goulash. Its specialty, however, is its corned beef sandwiches. Though you'll find Manny's surprisingly expensive, you won't argue with the quality. A corned beef sandwich will set you back seven smackers, but the thing is piled with meat and comes with the world's tastiest potato pancake and pickle. The potato pancake itself is almost worth the price.

HERITAGE DOWN HOME MUSIC

 1318 S. Halsted Street
Hours: Unpredictable

This grassroots shop specializes in blues cassettes, LPs, and CDs, but you'll find plenty of R&B and some rap mixed in. Nothing fancy, this is the type of shop that makes you feel like a jerk for occasionally frequenting places like Coconuts. The owner is deeply involved in the effort to save at least a portion of the Maxwell area from UIC. More than likely, however— barring some miracle change of heart on the part of the chancellor— there's a good chance this store will be gone in less than two years if not much sooner.

JIM'S

 1320 S. Halsted Street 312-666-0533
Hours: Open 24 hours

It doesn't get any more quintessentially Chicago than this. At this ratty little hot dog stand on the corner of Halsted and Maxwell, you'll find the best Polish sausage sandwich anywhere. This is not simply a fat hot dog on a bun, but a genuine bit of red, mottled, angry sausage. After simmering, this bad boy is charred, heaped with fried onions, and served on a bun with mustard. Two bucks and it's yours. But be careful, after a night of heavy drinking—when it goes down the best—this magnificent Polish tends to take its revenge. Make sure you're near comfortable bathroom facilities.

Pilsen, like the Maxwell Street area, is also the subject of controversy considering it too will be affected both by UIC's expansion and the city's plan for urban renewal. Pilsen was out of the Great Fire's path in 1871, and consequently a good portion of its buildings are more than 127 years old. Many of them are not in great shape, and as Pilsen serves as the arrival point for Mexican immigrants, the area is not exactly bursting with riches. In the old days German and Irish immigrants originally settled here and worked in the many nearby factories, but after the fire the area became predominantly Czech— or Bohemian, we should say, as Czechoslovakia didn't actually come into existence until after World War I. The neighborhood remained "respectable" up until the end of World War II, but then began declining as most of the Czech families left for the suburbs. Mexican immigrants began taking advantage of the cheap rents, and that process has continued to this day. So no, the overall economic status of Pilsen hasn't improved much over the decades, yet it's hardly "blighted" as the city contends. The western part of Pilsen is a loud, colorful place during the spring and sum-

PILSEN

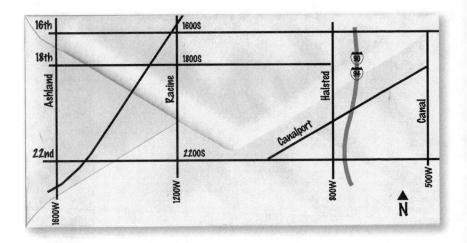

mer, where music leaks out onto the streets from the open doors of the shops and the bells dangling from the carts of the street vendors continually ring. Large murals are also splashed across a number of buildings.

To the east, things are different. Along Halsted a very white "artists" colony has sprung up over the years; a colony of which I myself am a resident. As this influx of whites has grown stronger recently, Mexican homeowners are afraid that their property taxes will soon grow to the point that a number of them will no longer be able to afford to remain in the area. Realistically, that is probably exactly what will happen. As every square foot of the north side in close proximity to the Loop gentrifies, more whites—both professionals as well as students and artists—are moving into the areas directly south of the Loop, where the process is being repeated. Though I only rent, I do feel a bit guilty at being a part of this wave. But then again, it's not like the Mexicans have been here forever—only since the '50s really, and as you've probably realized by now in reading this book, Chicago neighborhoods are always changing. Whether this is for better or worse, who's to say? It's simply the way it is.

LAWRENCE'S FISHERIES

 2120 S. Canal Street 312-225-2113
Hours: Open 24 hours

For my money, this is the best place to get fried shrimp in the city, not to mention catfish, seafood gumbo, scallops, frog legs, etc. Lawrence's is loud, crowded, and right off the river, but if you've got a hankering for some greasy fried seafood this is the place to go. There are a few tables but this is primarily a takeout joint. A great place to hit after a night of drinking.

LA ZACATECANA

 1722 S. Halsted Street
Hours: Mon–Sat, 10 A.M.–5 P.M.; closed Sun

This cluttered little junk shop is just that—a good old-fashioned, cluttered little junk shop. From old bicycles and washing machines to an occasional lawn mower, the merchandise is eclectic and often in less-than-tip-top shape. But, of course, you never know what you may find.

BIC'S HARDWARE CAFE

 1733 S. Halsted Street 312-850-2884
Hours: Sun–Thu, 7:30 A.M.–10 P.M.; Fri–Sat, 8:30 A.M.–12 A.M.

This coffee shop is part of the changing face of Pilsen. Once a Latino-owned hardware store, it now caters to the predominantly white artist crowd who live along this strip. A pleasant, laid-back, very unpretentious little joint, Bic's serves up some decent sandwiches and other edibles along with the joe.

LA COCINA

2028 S. Halsted Street 312-666-6863
Hours: Mon–Sat, 6 A.M.–7 P.M.; closed Sun

La Cocina is a matter of debate for many of the white artsy sorts familiar with it. Some are suspicious, advising to steer clear of meat dishes. Others swear by it—

some coming all the way from UIC to chow down. As for myself, I see no reason for any debate. What you get is a small taqueria serving up a small selection of decent food. Their breakfast menu is nicely varied, and I have to say the chicken gorditas are excellent. That annoying talking Chihuahua doesn't know what he's missing.

CUERNAVACA RESTAURANT

1158 W. Eighteenth Street 312-829-1147
Hours: Open every day 10 A.M.–11 P.M.

This is a very attractive Mexican restaurant, with high ceilings and a very impressive-looking bar. Although it's no taqueria, you can nonetheless order a plain old burrito for cheap; but full-on dinners are more their thing. These tend to be expensive, but the quality is first rate. There's actually a parking lot out front, making this one of the more convenient places to eat in Pilsen.

CAFE JUMPING BEAN

1439 W. Eighteenth Street 312-455-0019
Hours: Mon–Thu, 7:30 A.M.–10 P.M.; Fri, 7:30 A.M.–11 P.M.;
Sat, 8 A.M.–8 P.M.; Sun, 10 A.M.–6 P.M.

This colorful cafe serves as a meeting place for many of Pilsen's artists and activists. Pilsen's Mexican artists and activists, that is, rather than a white beachhead in the midst of the Mexican-owned groceries and shops. Here along with the coffee you can get some decent sandwiches and soup.

NUEVA LEON RESTAURANT

1515 W. Eighteenth Street 312-421-1517
Hours: Sun–Thu, 7 A.M.–11:30 P.M.; Fri–Sat, 7 A.M.–4 A.M.

Pilsen's best-known eatery, Nueva Leon is an upscale taqueria serving everything from taco plates to huge carne asada and guisado de puerco platters. Prices are reasonable and the atmosphere is very casual. The only major drawback is no beer. This can work in your favor if you're making a stop here after a night of drinking, but, if you're looking to knock back some chips and salsa and a spicy meal, be aware that you cannot do so with a cervaza fria. But remember, there's always carry-out.

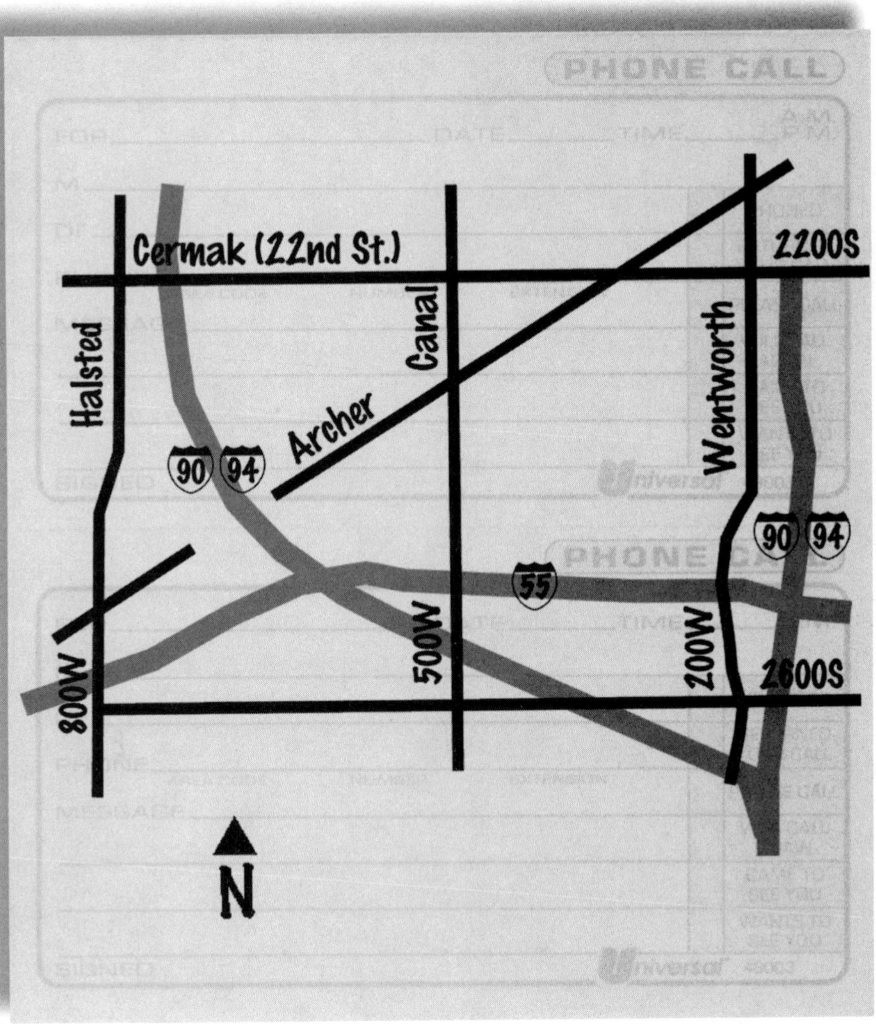

PHONE CALL
Cermak (22nd St.)
2200S
Halsted
Canal
Archer
Wentworth
90
94
90
94
55
800W
500W
200W
2600S
N

China Town sprang up just after the turn of the century. Pushed south by rising rents as well as racism, most Chinese immigrants were forced to settle in their present location in what was then the fringes of the red-light district—a neighborhood they certainly wouldn't have chosen on their own. Though the red-light district faded, China Town didn't begin to flourish until after World War II. Why, you ask? Well, it wasn't until 1943 that our ever-so-enlightened Congress repealed the Exclusion Act, which since 1882 had kept Chinese and other Asians from immigrating to the United States. It took the Japanese invasion of China and Southeast Asia to change Anglo sympathies. After the war a steady stream of immigrants began arriving, and with the advent of the Communist revolution in China, many of these immigrants were now skilled, educated, and well-to-do. By the '60s China Town was flourishing, filled with restaurants, shops, and laundries. These days an outdoor mall—China Town Square—was recently added, and a park along the river is in the works. Though the area isn't very large in square blocks, there is a large cluster of restaurants, groceries, and gift shops along Wentworth Avenue and in the Square.

WON KOW RESTAURANT

2237 S. Wentworth Avenue 312-842-7500
Hours: Sun–Thu, 9 A.M.–11 P.M.; Fri–Sat, 9 A.M.–12 A.M.

This place does a brisk business no matter what the time of year or day of the week. From beef to pork to chicken to seafood or even tofu, I've never had anything but a very tasty meal. Prices are reasonable, and their spicy dishes are perfect. Plus, if you can manage to go there with someone who can read Chinese, oh man, you'll get the works for cheap. This is the sort of place that's nice enough to bring your suburban parents to, but laid-back enough to show up in jeans or shorts. They also serve Dim Sum daily.

CHIU QUON BAKERY

2242 S. Wentworth Avenue 312-225-6608
Hours: Open every day 7 A.M.–9 P.M.

This little bakery has a great selection of bean and meat pastries as well as sweets for ridiculously cheap prices. You can order a sack full of stuff for only $5.

CHINA RESTAURANT

2253 S. Wentworth Avenue 312-225-2600
Hours: Mon–Thu, 4 P.M.–2 A.M.; Fri–Sat, 4 P.M.–3 A.M.;
Sun, 2 P.M.–2 A.M.

This dim, sedate little place first attracted me due to the tropical drinks advertised on their sign. And yes, the Dr. Fong drink may indeed have the cure for what ails you as the menu proclaims, but I'm a little more partial to the Mongolian Beef. They cook this stuff up right. As far as their other selections go, you probably won't achieve gastronomical ecstasy, but they definitely go down well. Never very crowded, this is a cool place to kick back for awhile and drink a few Tsing-Taos with your food.

SEVEN TREASURES

 2310 S. Wentworth Avenue 312-225-2668
Hours: Sun–Thu, 11 A.M.–2 A.M.; Fri–Sat, 11 A.M.–
2:30 A.M.

Large and brightly lit, this place can be a hazard to your eyes if you've just come from a dim bar, but late at night no one seems to mind—this place gets hopping. The menu is large and the portions huge, but your best bet is a noodle dish. Not only is this their specialty, but a big old bowlful is way cheap.

SHANGHAI RESTAURANT

2162 S. Archer Avenue 312-326-0077/326-0777
Hours: Open every day 10 A.M.–10 P.M.

Located in Chinatown Square, this brightly lit little restaurant serves up the most exquisite batch of Governor's Chicken I've ever had. Unfortunately they don't serve it with any sauce, but the breading and spices are out of this world. Other than this you can get an amazing variety of food—even casseroles. Dim Sum is served daily and the lunch specials are dirt cheap.

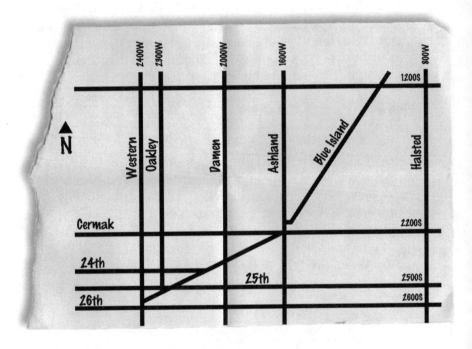

This is a very small area in Pilsen. Back before the 1920s, a large settlement of northern Italians from the Tuscany region settled here to work in the McCormick Reaper factory. Only a few blocks remain, but it is surprising amidst all the Mexican residents to suddenly come upon a handful of Italian restaurants and delis. Prices aren't cheap here, but if you're looking for some good Italian food, this is the place to be.

BRUNA'S RISTORANTE

2424 S. Oakley Avenue 773-254-5550
Hours: Mon–Thu, 11 A.M.–10 P.M.; Fri–
Sat, 11 A.M.–11 P.M.; Sun, 1 P.M.–10 P.M.

Serving up Northern Italian cuisine, Bruna's is definitely expensive, with pasta bowls going for $11 and entrées around $15. I must say, however, that if you don't mind spending some money, this is a great, intimate, comfortable little restaurant. And when I say pasta bowls, I mean bowls. The portions are huge and the food is outstanding.

LITTLE TUSCANY

MICELI'S DELI & FOODMART

2448 S. Oakley Avenue 773-847-6873
Hours: Mon–Fri, 8 A.M.–6:30 P.M.; Sat, 8 A.M.–4 P.M.;
closed Sun

This deli is a great place to get a sandwich or pick up various foodstuffs such as pasta, cheeses, and meats. They also have a great selection of Italian spices.

Bridgeport has been around for a long time—almost for as long as Chicago has officially been a city. Irish immigrants flocked here to work on the Illinois-Michigan Canal, establishing a shanty town in what soon became known as Bridgeport. Though the Irish weren't well received by the U.S.–born Yankees—one *Chicago Tribune* editorial declared they had smaller brains than your average Anglo-Saxon—they soon came to dominate the police force and the political system of Chicago. Bridgeport is still a very hard-nosed, working-class neighborhood, and from this base Richard J. Daley began his dynasty as Chicago mayor from 1955 to his death in 1976. His son, Richard M., now has the reign, and though his machine may be a bit more subtle, it is no less effective at keeping him and his people in office.

Bridgeport has made national news a few times due to racial incidents. Most notably, it was here that the Reverend Martin Luther King Jr. got pelted with a brick while leading a march through the neighborhood. Most recently Bridgeport was the scene of a nasty beating. Leonard Clark—a thirteen-year-old African-American boy—was beaten into a coma and brain-damaged by a

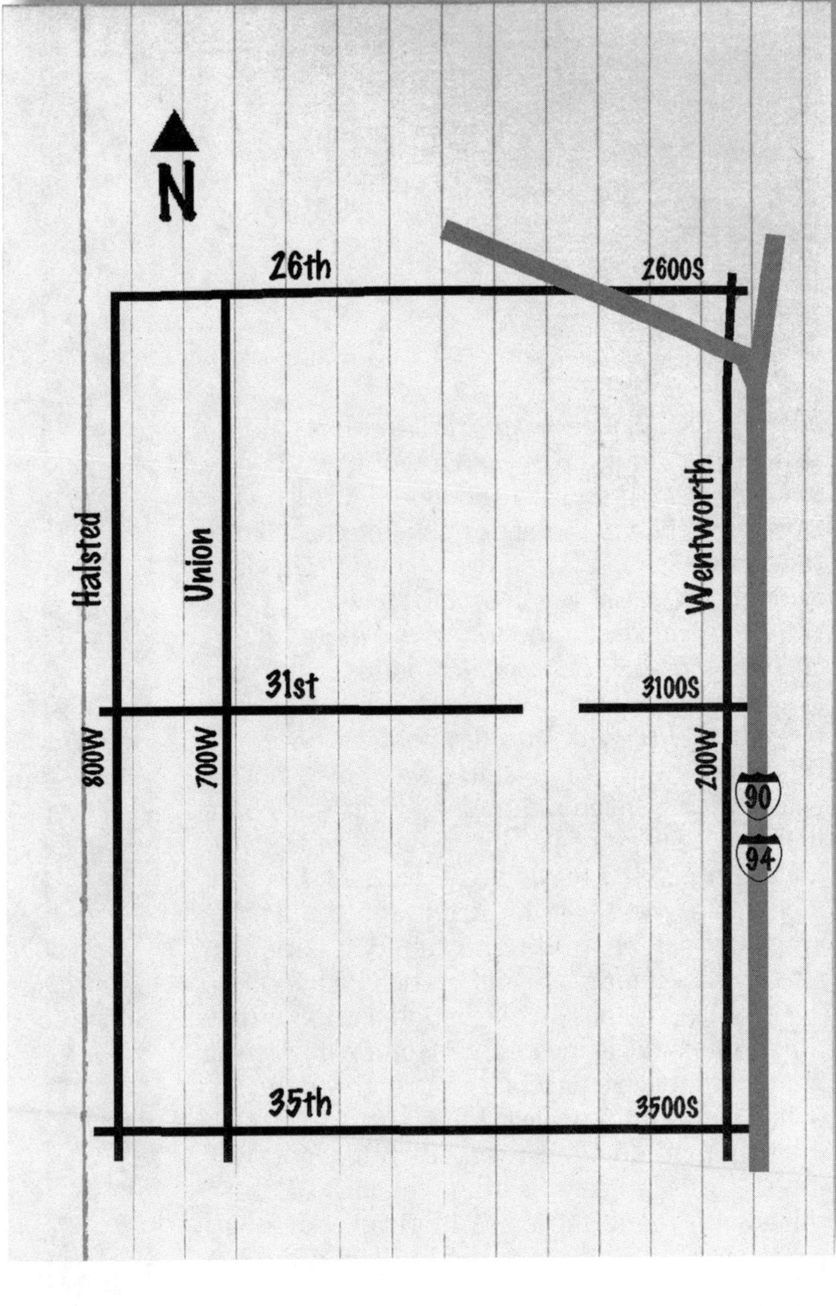
N
26th
2600S
Halsted
Union
Wentworth
31st
3100S
800W
700W
200W
90
94
35th
3500S

group of older white teenagers. The trial of one of these kids was delayed a number of times. Of the two witnesses, one was murdered in an "unrelated" robbery attempt, while the other disappeared in Arizona, only to re-surface after the trial. It's a tangled web.

But hell, Bridgeport isn't all that bad. Pilsen bumps right up to it and I often grocery shop here. It's also one of the best places to get yourself a Chicago-style hot dog as there are numerous stands in the area. Plenty of African-Americans, Latinos, and Chinese live here right alongside the whites. Pockets of the neighborhood, however, remain completely white. And I'm afraid that besides the one bar I mention, I'd advise against going into any bars if you're not white. Hell, I'd advise against going into any bars period. There's just something about drinking in a place where it's made highly obvious from the bartender on down that you're an unwelcome outsider that I don't find very appealing. When all talk ceases the moment you open the door, it's usually a good sign to turn right around and leave.

RICOBENE'S

252 W. 26th Street 312-225-5555
Hours: Mon–Thu, 11 A.M.–12:30 A.M.; Fri–Sat, 11 A.M.–
2 A.M.; Sun, 11:30 A.M.–12 A.M.

One of the south side's finest fast-food joints, Ricobene's serves up your typical burgers and pizza along with pasta and a variety of specialty sandwiches. The main attraction, however, is their Italian breaded steak sandwich. To the best of my knowledge, this sandwich is a purely (south side) Chicago invention, and Ricobene's does it up the best. What is an Italian breaded steak sandwich? Heaps of flank steak coated in breading, fried, then dumped on an Italian roll and covered in red sauce. Hot peppers and shredded mozzarella cheese are then slathered over it. It's one of the best damn sandwiches you'll ever have. And fully loaded it'll set you back less than $4. For non–meat eaters they make a tasty breaded eggplant sandwich. The fresh cut fries are excellent as well.

MAXWELL ST. DEPOT

411 W. Thirty-first Street 312-326-3514
Hours: Open 24 hours

Ever had a pork chop sandwich? Well, this is the place to get one. Slathered in fried onions, this puppy goes down well in the wee hours after a bender. It doesn't necessarily come out the other end as pleasantly the next day, but hell, every now and then it's worth it.

UNIQUE THRIFT STORE

3224 S. Halsted Street 312-842-8123
Hours: Mon–Sat, 9 A.M.–7 P.M.; Sun, 10 A.M.–5 P.M.

Unlike most of the Unique "chain," this one is bright, airy, and relatively untrampled. It's definitely worth your time to take a look here.

HEALTHY FOOD LITHUANIAN RESTAURANT

3236 S. Halsted Street 312-326-2724
Hours: Mon–Wed, 6:30 A.M.–4 P.M.; Thu–Sat, 6:30 A.M.–
8 P.M.; Sun, 7 A.M.–5 P.M.

A throwback to the days when Bridgeport was home to a number of Lithuanian immigrants around the turn of the century, Healthy Food is one of the most erroneously named restaurants I've ever frequented. They should rename it Hearty-Ass, Heart-Clogging Food. Along with standard American diner fare, you can also stuff down a number of traditional Lithuanian dishes such as blynai, which are pancakes served in a sort of "over easy" manner with your choice of fruit or cheese filling. The meat dumplings are good, but my favorite is the kugelis—a huge serving of potato pudding. Don't be intimidated by the waitress if she scoffs at you like you're a ninny if this is all you order. You probably won't even be able to finish it. The portions are gut-busting and the prices are cheap. As well, there's plenty of Lithuanian-themed paintings and carvings on the walls and various "objets d'art" for sale, including amber jewelry complete with trapped insects.

PUFFER'S

3356 S. Halsted Street 773-927-6073
Hours: Open every day 2 P.M.–2 A.M.

This small tavern is the only Northside-esque bar in Bridgeport; it's also the only bar in the neighborhood where you won't get the hairy eyeball upon entering. As mentioned before, lifelong Bridgeport residents tend to be very territorial when it comes to outsiders. Though the clientele at Puffer's is made up of many native Bridgeportians, the atmosphere here is very laid-back, friendly, and, surprisingly enough, bohemian. The owner loves music and you can usually catch a jam session most nights. There are also plenty of good beers on tap—this could be one of the only Bridgeport bars where you don't have to drink Old Style.

COMISKEY PARK

333 W. 35th Street 312-674-1000
Hours: Varies. Check paper or call ahead for game times.

Sure, the new stadium is very mall-like, the food is the same quality as convenience-store trash, and the beer (outside of what they serve at the bar in center field) is exclusively Miller Genuine Goat Piss or Lite, but hey, on Tuesdays through Thursdays you can gain admittance for only five bucks. This is supposed to relegate you to the Everest-like upper deck, but why bother when there are plenty of available seats in other parts of the stadium? I mean let's face it, the Sox haven't done too well since the days when Pearl Jam–pal Jack McDowell was on the mound. Consequently, you'll rarely find the park crowded. Plus, if you haven't been to a ballpark in a long time, you'll find it worthwhile. Sure you know some of those pitchers can throw

100 mph fast balls, but it's not until you're actually watching the guy live that you remember just how fast some of those balls can come flying from the mound. As well, you can usually find free street parking only a few blocks away. Even if you're not a baseball fan or into sports in general, you'll still find an afternoon or evening spent at the park quite worth it. Just don't wear any Cub paraphernalia. This is the South Side, ya mook, where people don't like dem Cubbies.

Nestled in the shadow of Cook County Jail, Little Village is a slightly more upscale version of Pilsen. It is to Little Village or the suburbs that many of Pilsen's residents finally move after saving up money for a house. Just like in Pilsen, Mexicans began replacing the original white ethnics in the 1950s. Many were stuck here until fairly recently as the suburbs to the west—namely Cicero—were notoriously racist. Though that situation has changed quite a bit, many homeowners have remained anyway. Here you'll find a long strip of restaurants, groceries, and shops catering primarily to the local clientele.

PUERTO MEXICO #2

3235 W. Twenty-sixth Street 773-247-4651
Hours: Open every day 8 A.M.–2 A.M.

This taqueria is a great place for take-out, though you can certainly kick back at a table if you so desire. Prices are cheap and the food is better than at many similar such joints. The tacos are particularly good—and tacos are not usually something I find myself recommending anywhere.

LITTLE VILLAGE

VILLAGE DISCOUNT OUTLET

4020 W. Twenty-sixth Street
Hours: Mon–Fri, 9 A.M.–9 P.M.; Sat, 9 A.M.–6 P.M.;
Sun, 11 A.M.–5 P.M.

Yes, they are everywhere. This one is bigger than most and slightly less picked over considering its out-of-the-way location. Still, I make no guarantees.

Hyde Park is known for the University of Chicago, one the country's most prestigious schools. Founded in 1892 near the lake in what was then a wealthy, primarily Jewish neighborhood, the university has continued to reside amid very desirable real estate. But know that this desirable real estate comprises only a few square blocks. Surrounding it is cheap, dilapidated housing occupied almost entirely by low-income African-Americans. There are, of course, plenty of affluent and middle-class African-Americans living among the whites in Hyde Park, but the contrast of the adjoining neighborhoods is impossible to miss. After the fall of the Berlin Wall, the *Chicago Reader* joked that Hyde Park had put in a bid to buy it for themselves.

Whatever the case, Hyde Park is definitely something to see, from its old houses and three-flats to the stately university buildings themselves. Just walking down the block makes you feel scholarly and Victorian. And it was here in Jackson Park by the lake that the World's Columbian Exposition took place in 1893. The building housing the Museum of Science and Industry was built for the fair, as well as a mock "White City" and the world's

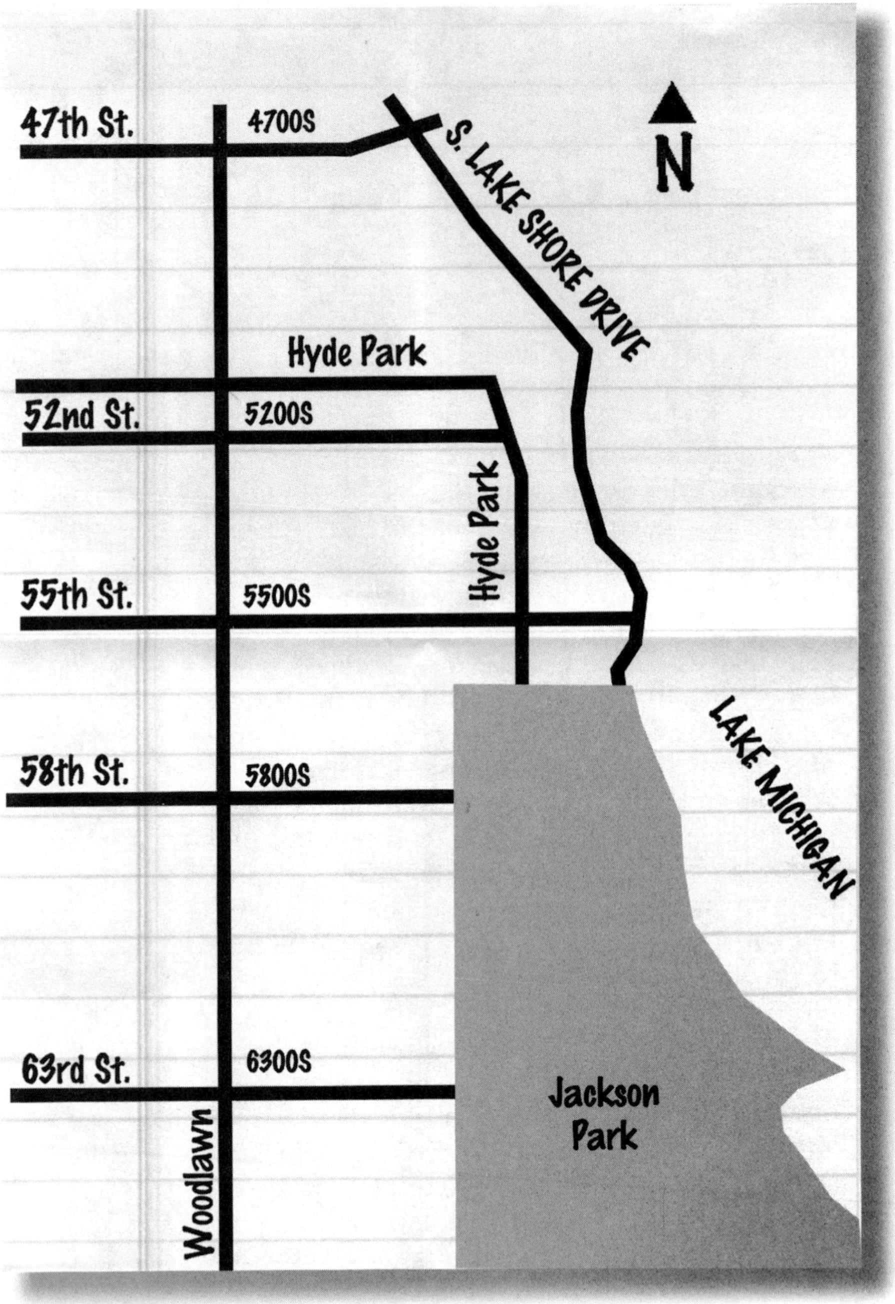

47th St.
4700S
S. LAKE SHORE DRIVE
N
Hyde Park
52nd St.
5200S
Hyde Park
55th St.
5500S
LAKE MICHIGAN
58th St.
5800S
63rd St.
6300S
Jackson Park
Woodlawn

first Ferris Wheel. Visitors to the event marveled at all the high-tech gadgets and innovations on display, much in the same way that we're impressed at electronic trade shows. So hey, even if you don't care about all the great bookstores in the neighborhood, at least come for the history.

DR. WAX

 5210 S. Harper 773-493-8696
Hours: Mon–Sat, 11 A.M.–8 P.M.; Sun, 12 P.M.–6 P.M.

Unlike its comfortably frumpy cousins up north, this is a sleek, upscale Dr. Wax. Though they do boast a small selection of vinyl, the primary stock is CDs. And rock is the secondary category here. R&B and jazz is the style du jour, only here you'll find mostly current artists. If this is your cup of tea, this is one of the better record shops in town.

SCHOLAR'S BOOKSTORE

 1379 E. Fifty-third Street 773-288-6565
Hours: Mon–Thu, 10 A.M.–6 P.M.; Fri–Sat, 10 A.M.–7 P.M.;
closed Sun

 This spartan, no-frills shop specializes in Chinese language books as well as English language books about China and Asia. They also sport a small fiction and martial arts section. In addition to books, they sell a large collection of Chinese videos as well as a number of used computer programs.

2ND HAND TUNES

 1377 E. Fifty-third Street 773-684-3375
Hours: Mon–Sat, 11 A.M.–7 P.M.; Sun, 11 A.M.–6 P.M.

This Hyde Park location stocks much more vinyl than CDs, and specializes in R&B and jazz rather than rock like the Clark Street store up north. Still, you can find plenty of rock at the usual decent prices. If you prefer R&B and jazz, however, you'll be quite pleased; their collection is very thorough.

THAI BUFFET

1638 E. Fifty-fifth Street 773-955-0911
Hours: Mon–Thu, 11:30 A.M.–10 P.M.; Fri–Sat,
11:30 A.M.–11 P.M.; Sun, 11:30 A.M.–9 P.M.

This place is great. From the time they open till 3 P.M. they offer an all-you-can-eat lunch buffet for only $5.69. Offerings include curry, pad Thai, Bangkok chicken, fried rice, and vegetable tempura to name but a few. The dinner buffet, from 5 to 9 every night, bests this with double the amount of entrées—sixteen of them, for only $6.99. Plus, it's completely self-service, from getting your own beverage to bussing your table, so you don't even have to worry about a tip. In the hours that the buffet isn't in effect, they offer a regular menu chock full of entrées. Cheap and tasty, this place is highly recommended.

JIMMY'S WOODLAWN TAP

1172 E. Fifty-fifth Street 773-643-5516
Hours: Mon–Fri, 10:30 A.M.–2 A.M.; Sat, 11 A.M.–3 A.M.;
Sun, 11:30 A.M.–2 A.M.

The Woodlawn Tap has been serving up the suds for over fifty years, and I wouldn't be surprised if in all that time the interior hasn't changed one bit. A very no-frills, well-worn shack of a joint, Jimmy's has simple beers on tap, simple sandwiches served up from the simple kitchen, and plenty of simple chairs and tables throughout the bar. The prices are pretty simple too. And this place doesn't just cater to the college folk, but quite an assortment of old-timers as well. Then again, maybe the latter were college folk some fifty years back and just can't bring themselves to leave. Whatever the case, this is a great, low-key place in which to down a few.

EX LIBRIS THEOLOGICAL BOOKS

1340 E. Fifty-fifth Street 773-955-3456
Hours: Mon–Fri, 12 P.M.–6 P.M.; Sat–Sun, 12 P.M.–5 P.M.

This used bookstore has an outstanding collection, with books ranging in topics from scholarly biblical studies to Buddhism, church histories, and sociological studies of various religions. The prices are very expensive, but then most of the volumes are from university presses. You're paying for their rarity as well. I mean let's face it, the average consumer isn't looking for a lengthy tome exploring the impact the concept of Satan has had on Western Culture, is he? Outside of a library, Ex Libris is pretty much the only place you're going to be lucky enough to find most of these titles.

POWELL'S BOOKSTORE

1501 E. Fifty-seventh Street 773-955-7780
Hours: Mon–Sun, 9 A.M.–11 P.M.

As is usually the case, this Powell's is a great place to spend hours browsing. Prices are cheaper here than in most used stores, and they even have a bargain basement with a smattering of fairly good titles. Their literature collection is first rate, as well as the Native American and history section. They also stock plenty of art and photography books. And if literary criticism is your thing (God help you), you'll be fit to be tied. Their collection of titles is enormous.

O'GARA & WILSON LTD.

1448 E. Fifty-seventh Street 773-363-0993
Hours: Mon–Sat, 9 A.M.–10 P.M.; Sun, 12 P.M.–10 P.M.

This immaculate, "old school" bookshop contains a good general selection of books, all of them in tip-top shape. Prices are a bit up there, but they have some great titles, especially when it comes to history. The section on the middle ages is particularly thorough. You can learn about everything from the Crusades to

Charlemagne's sex life. They say he was a man of great stature.

57TH STREET BOOKS

1301 E. Fifty-seventh Street 773-684-1300
Hours: Mon–Sat, 10 A.M.–10 P.M.; Sun, 10 A.M.–8 P.M.

This is one of the best stores selling new books in Chicago. In five brick, den-like rooms, you'll find a great collection of books. Everything from politics to children's picture books, literature to sci-fi is offered here, as well as quality periodicals. You may not find the latest self-help books or Tom Clancy novel, but good, thoughtful works from a large collection of publishers—both mainstream and independent. Various readings and workshops also take place here.

SEMINARY CO-OP BOOKSTORE

5757 S. University Avenue 773-752-4381
Hours: Mon–Fri, 8:30 A.M.–9 P.M.; Sat, 10 A.M.–6 P.M.;
Sun, 12 P.M.–6 P.M.

Located in the basement of the beautiful old Chicago Theological Seminary, this nationally known bookstore is a sprawling warren full of outstanding works. It is the Seminary Co-op that deserves the title of Chicago's best bookstore. It features thousands of new books with a heavy emphasis on scholarly works in the fields of sociology, history, and the humanities. You can literally spend hours here scanning all the different titles and still only scratch the surface of their inventory. No trip to Chicago is complete without at least one visit here. Expect to leave sweaty and content.

INFORMATION

If you're looking to see what particular bands are playing on any given night or what bar specials are being offered about town, there are a number of free publications in Chicago that will tell you just that. There are also a few online sources as well. Here are the best of them:

THE CHICAGO READER

Hands down the best free weekly publication in these here United States. Within the *Reader's* four thick and meaty sections you'll find great feature stories and articles, reviews, classifieds, and a comprehensive listing of what bands, art shows, movies, and plays are in town for the week. The *Reader* comes out on Thursdays and can be picked up just about anywhere on the North Side, from book and record stores to supermarkets.

BARFLY

This slim biweekly is your best source for the various specials bars will be offering throughout the week. It also features bar reviews and a number of articles of interest to the informed drunkard, such as the pros and cons of imbibing anything from tequila to Firewater. Available on every other Wednesday at many North Side book and record stores, as well as a number of bars.

THE ONION

Chicago is one of the few lucky cities to be treated to a free weekly print version of *The Onion*. This parody newspaper, which originates in Madison, Wisconsin, is not to be missed, although sometimes you'll need a strong stomach to put up with what can be borderline tasteless humor. To be honest, *The Onion* isn't going to tell you anything about what's going on in Chicago that the *Reader* and *Barfly* haven't already covered. But so what? It's one of the funniest papers you'll come across. While the second half of the paper is devoted to interviews and event listings, it's the first half you'll want to check out. If you haven't discovered *The Onion* yet in its print, on-line, or book form, trust me: you need to check it out. It comes out every Thursday and can be found in many North Side record and book stores, as well as a variety of vintage shops.

www.metromix.com

This Web site is the best of those devoted to Chicago happenings. It gives you information on everything from the weather and traffic patterns to what's going on in various restaurants and nightclubs. It also features plenty of articles on a variety of topics and you can also listen to demo tapes by local bands.

Two other web sites offering local information:

www.4chicago.com
www.chicago.sidewalk.com

GENERAL INDEX

A

Abraham Lincoln Bookshop, 17–18
Act I Bookstore, 68
Adam's Apple, 149
Adult Books, 58–59
African Wonderland Imports, 143–144
Afrocentric Bookstore, 12–13
Afterwords, 17
Agate Force, 77
Ajax Records, 44
Al's #1 Italian Beef, 168
Alley, The, a.k.a. The Alternative Shopping Complex, 98
American Indian Gift Store, 142–143
American Thrift Store, 31
Andersonville, 134–139
Ann Sather Restaurant, 136–137
Another Level/Lit X, 42
Arandas, 35
Arcanum Books and Curios, 115
Ark Thrift Shop, 23–24, 30, 77
Armadillo's Pillow, The, 157
Armaggedon, 84
Army & Navy Surplus, 75
Arriba Mexico, 76–77
Artful Dodger, 40
Arturo's, 45
Athenian Candle Company, 165
Atomic Cafe, 157
Augenblick, 124
Augusta Boulevard, 33–34
A–Z Wallis Military Surplus, 143

B

Back-a-Yard Restaurant, 108
Backseat Betty's, 26

Barbara's Bookstore, 58
Bargains Unlimited, 76
Bari Foods, 170
Batteries Not Included, 86
Beat Kitchen, 119
Beat Parlor, 43
Beatnix, 84
Belmont and Clark, 90–104
Belmont Army Surplus, 100
Berlin, 100
Bic's Hardware Cafe, 177
Big Horse, 27
Big John's Joint, 63
Bijou Theater, 58
Black Market Chicago, 23
Blast Off Video, 81
Blue Willow, 31–32
Bluebird Lounge, 51–52
Body Basics Precision Tattooing and Body Piercing, 81
Booklegger's Used Books, 81
Bookman's Corner, 66
Bookseller's Row, 10
Bookworks, The, 107
Borderline Tap, 38–39
Boys Town, 79–89
Bridgeport, 187–192
Brown Elephant Resale Shop, 88
Bruna's Ristorante, 185
Bucktown Pub, 41
Buddy Guy's Legends, 162
Bulldog Records, 24
Bundoo Khan Restaurant, 152
Burlesque Boutique, 37
BW-3 Sports Cafe & Pub, 68

C

Cafe Jumping Bean, 178
Caffe Pergolesi, 85
Casey's, 30
Chicago Antique Centre, 75
Chicago Architecture Foundation, 11
Chicago Avenue, 30–32
Chicago Comics, 95
Chicago Diner, 86
Chicago Music Exchange, 95
Chicago Recycle Shop, 138
Chicago Tattooing Company, The, 99
China Restaurant, 182
China Town, 180–183
Chiu Quon Bakery, 182
Chris and Heather's Record Roundup and Collectibles, 133
Christian Industrial League Resale Shop, 165
City Soles, 39
Club 950, 69
Clubfoot Lounge, 33
Clubhouse, The, 110
Clybourn Corridor, 51–55
Comic Relief, 12
Comiskey Park, 191–192
Crobar, 54
Crow's Nest Music, 13
Cuernavaca Restaurant, 178
Cupid's Treasure, 87–88

D

D & D Liquor, 36
Daily Bar & Grill, 128
Damen Avenue, 41–43
Dandelion, 43
Decibel Records, 76
Delilah's, 73
DeMar's, 31
Desert Treat, 103–104
Devon Avenue, 150–153
Diner Grill, 78
Disc Go Round, 67, 93

Disgraceland, 96
Division Street, 34–37
Doc Store, The, 94
Double Door, 29
Dr. Wax, 18, 64, 197
Duke of Perth, 66
Dusty Groove, 23

E

Earwax, 28
Egor's Dungeon, 99
El Chino, 25
El Yunqui Bookstore, 48
Elbo Room, 74
Elite Sportscard and Comics, 131
Empty Bottle, 44
Ennui Cafe, 157–158
Equator Club, 144
Estelle's, 40
Europa Bookstore, 18
Evil Clown Compact Disc, 85
Exchequer Pub, 12
Exit, 54–55
Ex Libris Theological Books, 199

F

Facets Multimedia Center, 66–67
Factory Theatre, The, 156
Falbo's Deli, 169
57th Street Books, 200
Fireside Bowl, 49
Flashback Collectibles, 107–108
Flashy Trash, 88
Frock Shop, The, 85
Funky Town, 103

G

Galaxy Comic Zone, 118
Gallery Bookstore, The, 83
Gandhi India Restaurant, 151
Garden Buffet, 148
Gate of Damascus Cafe, 129
Gaymart, 87
Ginger Man Tavern, The, 111
Gold Star, 35

Goso-Lo, 93
Gramaphone Ltd., 65
Grand Avenue, 170
Great Beer Palace, 125
Greciana Taverna, 128
Greektown, 163–166
Green Mill Lounge, 144

H

Hard Boiled Records and Video, 121
Healing Earth Resources and The
   Earth Cafe, 69
Healthy Food Lithuanian
   Restaurant, 190–191
Heartland Cafe, 158
Heritage Down Home Music, 174
Hi-Fi Records, 64
Hollywood Mirror, 96–97
Hot House, 162
Hubba-Hubba, 96
Hyde Park, 195–200

I

Innertown Pub, 34
Irazu, 29–30

J

Java Joe's, 89
Jazz Record Mart, 17
Jimmy and Tai's Wrigleyville Tap,
   109–110
Jimmy's Woodlawn Tap, 198
Jim's, 174

K

Kasia's Polish Deli, 32
Kingston Mines, 69
Kopi: A Traveler's Cafe, 139
Korea Restaurant, 148
Koreatown, 146–149

L

La Cocina, 177–178

Lakeview, 71–78
Land of the Lost, 84
Laurie's Planet of Sound, 129
Lava Lounge, 41
Lawrence Fisheries, 177
La Zacatecana, 177
Leathersport, 87
Le Garage, 43
Leona's Restaurant, 33–34, 101,
   156, 169
Leo's Lunchroom, 36
Liar's Club, 53
Lincoln Park, 61–70
Lincoln Park Bookshop, 64
Lincoln Square, 126–130
Little Italy, 167–170
Little Tuscany, 184–186
Little Village, 193–194
Logan Beach Cafe, 49–50
Logan Square, 46–50
Loop Records, 13
Loop, The, 8–13
Lounge Ax, 67–68
Lucky Buy/Second Time
   Around, 45

M

Mama Desta's Red Sea Ethiopian
   Restaurant, 93
Manny's Coffee Shop & Deli,
   173–174
Margie's Candies, 45
Mario's Lemonade Stand, 169
Martyr's, 123–124
Maxwell St. Depot, 190
Maxwell Street, 171–174
Maxwell Street Market, 173
Medusa's Circle, 95
Metro, 110
Meyer Delicatessen, 129
Miceli's Deli & Foodmart, 186
Mike's Broadway Cafe, 83
Milwaukee Avenue, 22–30
Moody's Pub, 145
Morseland Music Room, 159
Moti Mahal Indian Restaurant, 102

Mount Sinai Hospital Resale
    Shop, 70
Music Box Theatre, 115
Musician's Network, 139
Muskie's, 73–74, 101
Myopic Books, 35
Mystery Spot, The, 37

N

Nancy's, 79
Neo, 63
Never Mind, 83, 100
New Chinatown, 145
New World Resource Center, 48–49
New York Kosher Sausage
    Corporation, 153
Nhu Hoa Cafe, 145
Nick's, 26
99th Floor, 85
No Exit Cafe, The, 158
North Avenue, 37–41
North Center, 116–118
Note, The, 28
Nueva Leon Restaurant, 178–179
Nuts on Clark, 111

O

Occult Bookstore, 27
O'Gara & Wilson Ltd., 199-200
Old Town, 56–60
Old Town Ale House, 59–60
Old Town School of Folk Music, 128
Olive Tree Cafe, 136
Over 21 Bookstore, 58

P

Parthenon Restaurant, The, 166
Philly's Best, 97
Phyllis' Musical Inn, 36
Pick Me Up Cafe, 105–106
Pilsen, 175–179
Pink Frog, 98
Pippin's Tavern, 18
Pleasure Chest, The, 82
Pontiac Cafe, 42

Pop Era, 38
Pop's on Chicago, 32
Powell's Bookstore, 73, 162, 199
Prairie Avenue Bookshop, 11
Puerto Mexico #2, 193
Puffer's, 191

Q

Quake Collectibles, 115
Quaker Goes Deaf, The, 38
Quimby's Qveer Store, 37–38

R

Ragstock, 97
Rainbo Club, 42
Rain Dog Books, 10
Rand McNally Map & Travel
    Store, 16
Ravenswood, 131–133
Really Heavy Antiques, 136
Reckless Records, 27, 82
Record Emporium, 77–78
Record Exchange, 99, 159
Red Dog, 39
Revolution Books, 107
Reza's Restaurant, 138
Ricobene's, 189–190
Right Place, The, 137
River North, 14–18
Rocket 69, 92
Rogers Park, 154–159
Roscoe Village, 119–121
Russian-American Bookstore, The,
    152–153

S

Salvation Army Thrift Store, 25, 53,
    124, 139, 152
Sam's Wine and Liquors, 54
Sandmeyer's Bookstore, 161
Savvy Traveller, The, 11
Scholar's Bookstore, 197
Schuba's Tavern, 114
Second City Theatre, 59
2nd Hand Tunes, 65, 68, 197

See Hear Inc., 59
Selected Works Bookstore, 82–83
Seminary Co-op Bookstore, 200
Seven Treasures, 183
Shake Rattle and Read, 144–145
Shanghai Restaurant, 183
Shangrila, 120
Sheffield's Wine and Beer Garden, 101–102
Shiroi Hana Restaurant, 94–95
Simon's Tavern, 137
Smart Bar, 111
Smuggler's Row, 94
Sole Junkies, 92
Something Old Something New, 103
South Loop, 160–162
Southport, 112–115
Specialty Video, 137–138
St. Ben, 122–125
St. Vincent de Paul Thrift Store, 129–130
Stars Our Destination, The, 102
Stella Designs, 121
Stern's Books, 120–121
Strange Cargo, 107

T

Tai's Lounge, 78
Tecalitlan, 31
Thai Buffet, 198
Thai Lagoon, 40
Threads Etc., 24
Thurston's, 74
Topper's Recordtown, 143
Tragically Hip, 99–100
Tuman's Alcohol Abuse Center, 32
Turtle Island Books, 159
Two Doors South, 94

U

U.S. Government Bookstore, 12
Una Mae's Freak Boutique, 24
Unabridged Books, 82
Unan Imports, 157

Unique Thrift Store, 125, 143, 190
Untitled Aero, 66
Up Down Tobacco Shop, 59
Uptown, 140–145

V

Variety Comics, 118
Vibes Music, 156
Video Beat, 65
Village Discount Outlet, 48, 70, 121, 136, 148, 194

W

Wacky Cats, 76
Waxman Candles, 75
We're Everywhere, 86
Weeds, 53–54
West Town, 19–45
Western Avenue, 43–45
Why Not Cafe, 103
Wicker Dog, 29
Wild Hare & Singing Armadillo Frog Sanctuary, The, 109
Wisteria, 114–115
Women and Children First Bookstore, 138
Won Kow Restaurant, 182
Wrigley Field, 108
Wrigleyville, 105–112

X

Xoinx Tea Room, 74–75

Y

Yesterday, 109

Z

Zak's Tavern, 25
Ziggy's #1 Smoke & Novelty Shop, 64
Zorba's, 165–166

CATEGORY INDEX

ANTIQUES

Chicago Antique Centre, 75
Really Heavy Antiques, 136

ARMY SURPLUS

A–Z Wallis Military Surplus, 143
Army & Navy Surplus, 75
Belmont Army Surplus, 100

BAKERIES

Chiu Quon Bakery, 182

BARS

Bluebird Lounge, 51–52
Borderline Tap, 38–39
Bucktown Pub, 41
Delilah's, 73
Estelle's, 40
Ginger Man Tavern, The, 111
Gold Star, 35
Innertown Pub, 34
Lava Lounge, 41
Nick's, 26
Old Town Ale House, 59–60
Pippin's Tavern, 18
Rainbo Club, 42
Sheffield's Wine and Beer Garden, 101–102
Simon's Tavern, 137
Tai's Lounge, 78
Tuman's Alcohol Abuse Center, 32
Zak's Tavern, 25

BARS WITH FOOD

BW-3 Sports Cafe & Pub, 68
Big John's Joint, 63
Duke of Perth, 66

Exchequer Pub, 12
Great Beer Palace, 125
Jimmy and Tai's Wrigleyville Tap, 109–110
Jimmy's Woodlawn Tap, 198
Moody's Pub, 145

BARS WITH LIVE MUSIC

Augenblick, 124
Phyllis' Musical Inn, 36
Pop's on Chicago, 32
Puffer's, 191
Weeds, 53–54

BARS WITH FOOD AND LIVE MUSIC

Big Horse, 27
Empty Bottle, 44

BOOKSTORES, NEW

57th Street Books, 200
Act I Bookstore, 68
Afrocentric Bookstore, 12–13
Barbara's Bookstore, 58
Chicago Architecture Foundation, 11
Lincoln Park Bookshop, 64
Prairie Avenue Bookshop, 11
Quimby's Qveer Store, 37–38
Sandmeyer's Bookstore, 161
Seminary Co-op Bookstore, 200
Stars Our Destination, The, 102
Stern's Books, 120–121
U.S. Government Bookstore, 12
Unabridged Books, 82
Women and Children First Bookstore, 138

BOOKSTORES, USED

Armadillo's Pillow, The, 157
Booklegger's Used Books, 81
Bookman's Corner, 66
Bookseller's Row, 10
Bookworks, The, 107
Gallery Bookstore, The, 83
Myopic Books, 35
O'Gara & Wilson Ltd., 199-200
Powell's Bookstore, 73, 162, 199
Rain Dog Books, 10
Selected Works Bookstore, 82–83
Shake Rattle and Read, 144–145

BOOKSTORES, NEW AND USED

Abraham Lincoln Bookshop, 17–18
Afterwords, 17
Ex Libris Theological Books, 199
New World Resource Center, 48–49
Revolution Books, 107
Scholar's Bookstore, 197

BOOKSTORES, NEW AGE/OCCULT

Arcanum Books and Curios, 115
Occult Bookstore, 27
Turtle Island Books, 159

BOOKSTORES, FOREIGN LANGUAGE

El Yunqui Bookstore, 48
Europa Bookstore, 18

CANDLES

Athenian Candle Company, 165
Waxman Candles, 75

CLOTHING

Le Garage, 43
Medusa's Circle, 95
Never Mind, 83, 100
99th Floor, 85
Pink Frog, 98
Untitled Aero, 66
We're Everywhere, 86

CLUBS

Artful Dodger, 40
Berlin, 100
Club 950, 69
Clubfoot Lounge, 33
Crobar, 54
Equator Club, 144
Exit, 54–55
Liar's Club, 53
Neo, 63
Red Dog, 39
Smart Bar, 111

CLUBS WITH LIVE MUSIC

Double Door, 29
Elbo Room, 74
Fireside Bowl, 49
Green Mill Lounge, 144
Hot House, 162
Lounge Ax, 67–68
Martyr's, 123–124
Metro, 110
Morseland Music Room, 159
Note, The, 28
Wild Hare & Singing Armadillo Frog
  Sanctuary, The, 109

CLUBS WITH LIVE MUSIC AND FOOD

Beat Kitchen, 119
Buddy Guy's Legends, 162
Heartland Cafe, 158
Kingston Mines, 69
Schuba's Tavern, 114
Thurston's, 74

COFFEE SHOPS

Atomic Cafe, 157
Bic's Hardware Cafe, 177
Cafe Jumping Bean, 178
Caffe Pergolesi, 85
Earwax, 28
Ennui Cafe, 157–158
Java Joe's, 89
Kopi: A Traveler's Cafe, 139
Logan Beach Cafe, 49–50

No Exit Cafe, The, 158
Pick Me Up Cafe, 105–106
Why Not Cafe, 103
Xoinx Tea Room, 74–75

COMIC BOOK SHOPS

Chicago Comics, 95
Comic Relief, 12
Elite Sportscard and Comics, 131
Galaxy Comic Zone, 118
Variety Comics, 118
Yesterday, 109

DELIS

Bari Foods, 170
Falbo's Deli, 169
Kasia's Polish Deli, 32
Meyer Delicatessen, 129
Miceli's Deli & Foodmart, 186

FAST FOOD

Al's #1 Italian Beef, 168
Jim's, 174
Lawrence Fisheries, 177
Maxwell St. Depot, 190
Muskie's, 73–74, 101
Philly's Best, 97
Ricobene's, 189–190
Wicker Dog, 29

FOOTWEAR

City Soles, 39
Doc Store, The, 94
Sole Junkies, 92

HEAD SHOPS

Adam's Apple, 149
Egor's Dungeon, 99
Ziggy's #1 Smoke & Novelty Shop, 64

HIPSTER BOUTIQUES

Agate Force, 77
Alley, The, a.k.a. The Alternative
    Shopping Complex, 98
Another Level/Lit X, 42
Gaymart, 87

Pop Era, 38
Rocket 69, 92
Smuggler's Row, 94
Two Doors South, 94

LIQUOR STORES

Casey's, 30
D & D Liquor, 36
Sam's Wine and Liquors, 54

MUSIC/RECORD STORES

Ajax Records, 44
Armaggedon, 84
Beat Parlor, 43
Bulldog Records, 24
Chicago Music Exchange, 95
Chris and Heather's Record
    Roundup and Collectibles, 133
Clubhouse, The, 110
Crow's Nest Music, 13
Decibel Records, 76
Disc Go Round, 67, 93
Dr. Wax, 18, 64, 197
Dusty Groove, 23
Evil Clown Compact Disc, 85
Gramaphone Ltd., 65
Heritage Down Home Music, 174
Hi-Fi Records, 64
Jazz Record Mart, 17
Laurie's Planet of Sound, 129
Loop Records, 13
Musician's Network, 139
Old Town School of Folk Music, 128
Quaker Goes Deaf, The, 38
Reckless Records, 27, 82
Record Emporium, 77–78
Record Exchange, 99, 159
2nd Hand Tunes, 65, 68, 197
See Hear Inc., 59
Topper's Recordtown, 143
Vibes Music, 156

RESALE SHOPS

American Thrift Store, 31
Ark Thrift Shop, 23–24, 30, 77
Bargains Unlimited, 76
Brown Elephant Resale Shop, 88

Chicago Recycle Shop, 138
Christian Industrial League Resale
    Shop, 165
La Zacatecana, 177
Lucky Buy/Second Time Around, 45
Mount Sinai Hospital Resale Shop,
    70
Right Place, The, 137
Salvation Army Thrift Store, 25, 53,
    124, 139, 152
Something Old Something New, 103
St. Vincent de Paul Thrift Store,
    129–130
Unique Thrift Store, 125, 143, 190
Village Discount Outlet, 48, 70, 121,
    136, 148, 194

RESTAURANTS

Chinese
Blue Willow, 31–32
China Restaurant, 182
Seven Treasures, 183
Shanghai Restaurant, 183
Won Kow Restaurant, 182

Costa Rican
Irazu, 29–30

Diners
Daily Bar & Grill, 128
DeMar's, 31
Diner Grill, 78
Manny's Coffee Shop & Deli,
    173–174
Mike's Broadway Cafe, 83

Ethiopian
Mama Desta's Red Sea Ethiopian
    Restaurant, 93

Greek
Greciana Taverna, 128
Parthenon Restaurant, The, 166
Zorba's, 165–166

Indian
Gandhi India Restaurant, 151
Moti Mahal Indian Restaurant, 102

Italian
Bruna's Ristorante, 185
Leona's Restaurant, 33–34, 101, 156,
    169
Nancy's, 79

Jamaican
Back-a-Yard Restaurant, 108

Japanese
Shiroi Hana Restaurant, 94–95

Korean
Garden Buffet, 148
Korea Restaurant, 148

Lithuanian
Healthy Food Lithuanian
    Restaurant, 190–191

Mexican
Arandas, 35
Arriba Mexico, 76–77
Arturo's, 45
Cuernavaca Restaurant, 178
El Chino, 25
La Cocina, 177–178
Nueva Leon Restaurant, 178–179
Puerto Mexico #2, 193
Tecalitlan, 31

Middle Eastern/Mediterranean
Desert Treat, 103–104
Gate of Damascus Cafe, 129
Olive Tree Cafe, 136
Reza's Restaurant, 138

Swedish
Ann Sather Restaurant, 136–137

Thai
Thai Buffet, 198
Thai Lagoon, 40

Vegetarian/Healthy
Chicago Diner, 86
Leo's Lunchroom, 36
Pontiac Cafe, 42

Vietnamese
Nhu Hoa Cafe, 145

SEX SHOPS

Adult Books, 58–59
Batteries Not Included, 86
Black Market Chicago, 23
Cupid's Treasure, 87–88
Leathersport, 87
Over 21 Bookstore, 58
Pleasure Chest, The, 82

SMOKE SHOPS

Up Down Tobacco Shop, 59

STADIUMS

Comiskey Park, 191–192
Wrigley Field, 108

SWEETS

Margie's Candies, 45
Mario's Lemonade Stand, 169
Nuts on Clark, 111

TATTOO PARLORS

Body Basics Precision Tattooing and
    Body Piercing, 81
Chicago Tattooing Company,
    The, 99

THEATERS

Bijou Theater, 58
Facets Multimedia Center, 66–67
Factory Theatre, The, 156
Music Box Theatre, 115
Second City Theatre, 59

TRAVEL SHOPS

Rand McNally Map & Travel
    Store, 16
Savvy Traveller, The, 11

VIDEO STORES

Blast Off Video, 81
Hard Boiled Records and Video, 121
Specialty Video, 137–138
Video Beat, 65

VINTAGE/RETRO SHOPS

Backseat Betty's, 26
Beatnix, 84
Burlesque Boutique, 37
Dandelion, 43
Flashback Collectibles, 107–108
Flashy Trash, 88
Frock Shop, The, 85
Funky Town, 103
Goso-Lo, 93
Hollywood Mirror, 96–97
Hubba-Hubba, 96
Land of the Lost, 84
Mystery Spot, The, 37
Quake Collectibles, 115
Ragstock, 97
Shangrila, 120
Stella Designs, 121
Strange Cargo, 107
Threads Etc., 24
Tragically Hip, 99–100
Una Mae's Freak Boutique, 24
Wacky Cats, 76
Wisteria, 114–115

ABOUT THE AUTHOR

Bill Franz was born in suburban Chicago, and but for two brief sojourns in New Orleans has lived in the city itself for thirteen years. A graduate of Columbia College with a degree in creative writing, he has worked a variety of jobs as he has pursued a writing career. Currently, he works as an educator in the Chicago public school system.